The Historical Christ
and the Theological Jesus

The Historical Christ
and the Theological Jesus

Dale C. Allison, Jr.

WILLIAM B. EERDMANS PUBLISHING COMPANY
GRAND RAPIDS, MICHIGAN

Wm. B. Eerdmans Publishing Co.
2140 Oak Industrial Drive N.E., Grand Rapids, Michigan 49505
www.eerdmans.com

Library of Congress Cataloging-in-Publication Data

Allison, Dale C.
The historical Christ and the theological Jesus / Dale C. Allison, Jr.
p.   cm.
Includes bibliographical references.
ISBN 978-0-8028-6262-4 (pbk.: alk. paper)
1. Jesus Christ — Historicity. 2. Jesus Christ — History of doctrines.
I. Title.

BT303.2.A545 2009
232.9'08 — dc22

2008046908

For Ron Tappy

In friendship

ישבעו עצי יהיה ... אשר־שם צפרים יקננו

Contents

PREFACE   ix

INTRODUCTION: A Brief Overview   1

1. The Problem of Theological Utility   6
    The Enduring Discord of the Experts   8
    The Enduring Challenge of Personal Predilection   15
    The Perceptions of Others and Personal Identity   22

2. Disputed Questions   31
    How Much History Does Theology Require?   32
    How Should We Treat Our Texts?   40
    How Might One Come to Know Jesus?   45

3. How to Proceed   53
    The Wrong Tools for the Wrong Job   54
    The General and the Particular   61
    Miracles Here, There, and Everywhere   66

4. Some Difficult Conclusions   79
    Christology: Too Low and Too High   80
    Eschatology: Here to Stay   90
    Context: Gone for Good   101

5. Some Personal Impressions   104

   Contradiction: Divine Love and Human Woe   105

   Imagination: Ought over Is   113

   Synthesis: The Coincidence of Opposites   116

INDEX OF MODERN NAMES   120

INDEX OF SCRIPTURE   122

Preface

I have, for many years now, involved myself in the so-called quest of the historical Jesus. During most of that time, the religious implications of my activities have been at the margin of my awareness. Despite being a lifelong churchgoer, my self-conception has usually been that of a historian writing to historians, not of a Christian writing to Christians. Moved by curiosity and the attendant joy of discovery, and desiring to evaluate the evidence honestly, whatever the outcome, I have sought to learn, through historical-critical methods, what I can about the first-century Jew Jesus of Nazareth.

I have never been without theological motives or interests. Until a few years ago, however, I had not attempted to pursue those interests with much diligence or to examine my motives with much care. Recent circumstances have pushed me out of my historical-critical pose. After accepting a teaching post at a Protestant theological seminary, I soon discovered that future pastors are not interested in undertaking historical labor without the prospect of theological reward. In order, then, to keep my audience, I was compelled to complement my critical inquiries with theological deliberations.

Sustained theological reflection also became incumbent when I accepted an invitation to join a research group at the Center of Theological Inquiry in Princeton, a group dedicated to discussing "the identity of Jesus."[1] The participants included not only well-known biblical scholars —

---

1. Papers produced for that group are now collected in Beverly Gaventa and Richard Hays, eds., *Seeking the Identity of Jesus* (Grand Rapids, MI: Eerdmans, 2008).

Gary Anderson, Markus Bockmuehl, Beverly Gaventa, Kathy Grieb, Richard Hays, Joel Marcus, Walter Moberly, Marianne Meye Thompson, and Francis Watson — but also prominent theologians and historians of doctrine — Sarah Coakley, Brian Daley, Robert Jenson, Bill Placher, Katherine Sonderegger, and David Steinmetz. Sitting around the table with these engaging folk enabled me to develop thoughts that had theretofore remained only embryonic and to jettison others that failed to endure critical scrutiny. I am grateful for all they have taught me and encouraged me to ponder.

I wrote this book in preparation for the Kenneth W. Clark lectures, which I delivered at Duke University in February of 2008, and I should like to thank Douglas Campbell, Stephen Carlson, Susan Eastman, Richard Hays, Joel Marcus, Jacquelyn Norris, and Kavin Rowe for their hospitality on that occasion. This book retains the informal character of my oral presentations. Joel has also kindly read and commented on parts of the manuscript, as have Kathy Anderson, Chris Kettler, Nancy Klancher, Tom Meredith, two of my children, Emily and John, and my wife, Kristine. I have tried to be their student.

A Brief Overview

"One does not solve this problem. One can only bear witness to it."

RICHARD GALE

"It may be necessary to live with uncertainty as an alternative to living with a closed mind."

DAVID HAY

For almost seventeen hundred years, Christians regarded the four canonical Gospels as being, among other things, records of what actually happened. Divine inspiration seemed to guarantee historical veracity, as did the belief that the purported authors of those Gospels, Matthew, Mark, Luke, and John, were either eyewitnesses or friends of eyewitnesses. An additional reason for trust was the supposition that the evangelical stories fulfill many of the messianic oracles in the Jewish Bible. The upshot was the conviction that Jesus said and did everything that the Gospels have him say and do. To read them was to encounter him as he once walked upon the earth.

There were, to be sure, moderating voices. Some, such as the church fathers Papias and Jerome, were fully aware that the Gospels do not agree on the order in which events happened. So too the medieval Syriac commentator Dionysius bar Salibi and the sixteenth-century Spanish exegete Maldonatus. The latter observed that "the Evangelists, like the other biblical authors, do not follow chronological order" and further that the discourses of Jesus "neither report all that he said nor quote him in the order in which he spoke."[1] Luther thought that Mark 13, the eschatological discourse, is a bit misleading because it does not preserve the order of the words as Jesus spoke them.

John Calvin also sat loose on some things. He recognized, for instance, that Matthew 5–7, the Sermon on the Mount, and Matthew 10, the Missionary Discourse, are secondary compilations. According to Calvin, the First Evangelist, for thematic reasons, gathered into his discourses words that at one time were scattered, words that Jesus originally uttered on diverse occasions.[2]

Even more clear-eyed was Origen, who in the third century anticipated modern criticism by candidly observing that at "many points" the four Gospels "do not agree." He inferred that their truth cannot reside in "the material letter." The Evangelists "sometimes altered things which, from the eye of history, occurred otherwise." They could "speak of something that happened in one place as if it had happened in another, or of what happened at a certain time as if it had happened at another time," and they introduced "into what was spoken in a certain way some changes of their own." "The spiritual truth was often preserved, one might say, in the material falsehood."[3]

Despite the observations of Origen and a few other attentive readers, serious doubt over the historical fidelity of the canonical Gospels never, to my knowledge, assailed anyone in the ancient or medieval church.

Outside the church, there was more than doubt. Jews who disbelieved in Jesus as their promised Messiah did not, if the subject came up, credit the Christian stories about him. We accordingly find that old Jewish sources offer polemical alternatives. Surely Jesus must have been, as the Babylonian Talmud has it, a deceiver, a fraud who deliberately led Israel astray, and his followers must have been of the same unscrupulous

---

1. Juan Maldonatus, *Comentarii in Quatuor Evangelistas* (2 vols.; London/Paris: Moguntiae, 1853-54), 1:59. For Papias see Eusebius, *Ecclesiastical History* 3.39.15. Jerome's remarks, which depend on Papias, appear in his *Commentary on Matthew* Preface 30. For Dionysius bar Salibi see his *Explication of the Gospels.*.

2. John Calvin, *A Harmony of the Gospels Matthew, Mark and Luke,* vol. 1 (Grand Rapids, MI: Eerdmans, 1972), pp. 168, 297. When remarking on the differences between Matt. 4:5-11 and Luke 4:5-13, Calvin observed: "the Evangelists had no intention of so putting their narrative together as always to keep an exact order of events" (p. 139).

3. Origen, *Commentary on John* 10.2, 4.

character (*Sanhedrin* 43a). Already Matt. 28:11-15 reports that "the Jews" circulate a tale, originally concocted in desperation, in which the disciples, coming by night, steal their master's body. The later *Toledoth Jesu,* a medieval Jewish collection that purports to offer the real story behind the Christian stories, gives us more of the same: Mary was impregnated by a Roman soldier, Jesus was a magician in league with demonic hosts, the disciples staged the resurrection, and so on.

The contradictory alternatives of the Christian apologists and their Jewish antagonists no longer exhaust the options for readers of the Gospels. A series of historic developments — the critical study of texts initiated during the Renaissance, the Protestant critiques of Roman Catholic tradition, the growing secularism in the wake of the wars of religion, and the skepticism of tradition that attended the Enlightenment — conspired to fashion new ways of understanding the Scriptures, not only outside the churches but also within them; and those new ways eventually led, perhaps inevitably, to the modern quest for the historical Jesus.

The story of that quest's birth in the eighteenth century and of its various manifestations in the nineteenth century found its most famous chronicler in Albert Schweitzer, whose wonderfully entertaining narrative has instructed so many about Hermann Samuel Reimarus, Heinrich Eberhard Gottlob Paulus, David Friedrich Strauss, and Johannes Weiss.[4] We also now have some first attempts to narrate the progress, if that is the right word, of the quest during the twentieth century, only recently passé.[5] So the author of the present book need not become a cartographer of the discipline. My subject is rather another: What are the religious implications of the quest?

Remarkably, many pew-sitters are happily oblivious of what has been going on in the thinking world for two and a half centuries. They have somehow avoided most or even all of the serious intellectual commentary on the Gospels since the Enlightenment. Perhaps typical are the two churches I grew up in, one Presbyterian, one Congregationalist. Never in Sunday School or from the pulpit did I hear anything of the modern debates surrounding Jesus and the Gospels.

---

4. Albert Schweitzer, *The Quest of the Historical Jesus,* first complete edition (Minneapolis: Fortress, 2000). The first German edition appeared in 1906.

5. Especially useful is Walter P. Weaver, *The Historical Jesus in the Twentieth Century, 1900-1950* (Harrisburg, PA: Trinity Press Intl., 1999).

Ignorance, it is said, is voluntary misfortune. Still, one expects something from one's teachers. Either my pastors knew nothing about the debates regarding Jesus, or they consciously kept a convenient silence. Perhaps they were persuaded that their congregants did not need to know what they knew, and maybe they worried that curiosity might kill the Christian. I recall that Maldonatus says somewhere: "It is a duty for us to doubt for others, lest they doubt for themselves." In any case, my pastors failed one inquisitive teenager miserably. I had to stumble onto the almost invisible topic all on my own, without help from the church, and then I had to wonder, sitting alone in my bedroom, Why all the secrecy?

Once I began to read the literature, I suffered theological confusion and anxiety, as must many churchgoers today when they learn of the quest for the first time through National Public Radio or *Time Magazine,* or when they browse the offerings of a bookstore, stumble onto the various titles about Jesus, and then actually read a couple. Once becoming aware of this strange new world of the critical historians, Christians may well worry whether the quest is a subject that they can, having learned about it, safely ignore, or whether it instead confronts them with facts that should amend, perhaps significantly, their inherited religious convictions.

They may, for instance, fret upon learning that many modern scholars do not believe that Matthew wrote Matthew or that Jesus spoke the discourses in John. They may also, depending on their background, find themselves vexed upon becoming persuaded that the old props — miracles, eyewitness origins, the proof from prophecy — have seemingly fallen to the ground and are in need of being themselves propped up or maybe abandoned as everlasting ruins. Such individuals have awakened from their dogmatic slumbers and cannot go back to sleep. I find myself among them. I do not long for that old-time religion, nor do I wish to believe in my own belief but, as quaint as this may sound to some, I want to know the truth, even if I cannot cheer it.

Recently I received a poignant letter from a graduate student in a prestigious department of religion in the United States. Among his sentences were these:

The more I study the Gospels and the life of Jesus (my two main areas of interest), the more I become convinced that quite a few of the convictions of "orthodox" Christianity are really wistful illusions. Though there is hardly time (nor need) to go into the dozens and dozens (quite literally, as I have little doubt you know from personal experience) of historical, theological, and philosophical conundrums surrounding Jesus and the NT, I find myself often extremely disturbed by the implications of these (often) intractable dilemmas. Perhaps this is partly because I entered the community of faith "through an evangelical door" while in college (I am, however, no longer "evangelical" in the traditional sense of that term), but I believe it is predominantly because I am a fairly thoughtful Christian, and I can't get rid of the cognitive dissonance that festers within the mind and heart of one who wants to "believe in and serve God through Jesus" while at the same time doubting that there "even is a God and/or a Jesus" who still "works in the world" today. . . . I am sorry to have written so much, but this stuff floods my mind morning to night, and it has become increasingly difficult to live a life of commitment to Christ in the face of these doubts.

How should I have addressed this man's concerns, which included doubts about Jesus' resurrection as well as perplexity that Jesus did not expect ordinary history to march on much longer? My response was necessarily inadequate. I offered that there are no obvious or easy answers to the complex issues that historical criticism raises for Christians, that there is nothing for us but lots of hard thinking. One should be conscientious and open-minded, willing to be disturbed by arguments, and ready, when necessary, to sweep some things into the dustbin of one's personal past.

What has become of my anxious letter-writer I do not know. But if he were to write to me today, I would refer him to this book, in which I have set forth, as best as I am able, some of the tentative conclusions I have reached after years of study. It is my personal testimony to doubt seeking understanding.

Whatever one makes of the following pages, they are the stammerings neither of an apologist nor of a skeptic but instead of an oft-confused Protestant who has come to his conclusions, modest as they are, quite gradually, and who may alter his uncertain mind about much tomorrow. Of two things only do I feel assured. The first is that, as unchanging things do not grow — rocks remain rocks — informed changes of mind should be welcomed, not feared. The second is this: the unexamined Christ is not worth having.

CHAPTER 1

The Problem of Theological Utility

"It is an emotional necessity to exalt the problem to which one wants to devote a lifetime."

EUGENE WIGNER

"I believe there are visions that come to us only in memory, in retrospect. That's the pulpit speaking, but it's telling the truth."

MARILYNNE ROBINSON

Of what use, if any, is the so-called historical Jesus for Christian theology? The question is not rhetorical but sincere, the answer not obvious but obscure. I suppose that, in one way or another, I have been struggling with the problem for decades; and the longer I have thought, the more convoluted and challenging everything has become. Like all the other nontrivial questions in this vale of tears, the arguments are many, the conclusions few.

Others have been more self-assured of their ability to see the truth in this matter. The late Robert Funk, who spent the last twenty years of his life earnestly promoting the Jesus Seminar, believed that his historical researches and those of his like-minded coworkers were of immense theological import.[1] Critical study, he stridently argued, demonstrates

---

1. For what follows see Robert W. Funk, *Honest to Jesus: Jesus for a New Millenniuim* (San Francisco: HarperSanFrancisco, 1996).

beyond a reasonable doubt that Jesus was not born of a virgin, that he did not make himself out to be God's unique Son, and that his body did not escape nature's recycling process. It is time, insisted Funk, to grow up, to discard the orthodox fairy tales, and to recognize that Christians have been captive to a false religion, from which knowledge of Jesus of Nazareth as he really was will set us free. Honesty before the facts compels us to swap our obsolete creeds for a new ideology inspired by the real, the historical, the non-Christian Jesus. We cannot serve both the historian's Jesus and the church's Christ.

Funk's position is not idiosyncratic. John Dominic Crossan has asserted that "reconstructing the historical Jesus" is "a way of doing necessary open-heart surgery on Christianity itself."[2]

Even scholars more sympathetic with traditional Christian convictions have in principle concurred on the fundamental theological significance of the quest for the historical Jesus. Joachim Jeremias, whose Jesus is so unlike Funk's Jesus, also believed that theologians should, in principle, heed historians. Not only is conscientious study of the historical Jesus a bulwark against modernizing ideologies but, for Jeremias, the incarnation demands that we seek to understand, as best we can, the flesh-and-blood Jesus of Nazareth. God became incarnate not in a text but in a human life, from which it follows that Christians are obligated to inquire beyond and behind the canonical texts, impelled to learn all that they can about a first-century Galilean Jew.[3]

One understands Jeremias's conviction. Might not the pursuit of the pre-canonical Jesus help us to distinguish between him and our distorted images of him? Might not historical study shed helpful light on what Jesus really said and did?

Funk and Jeremias represent those who insist that the historians be seated at the theological table. Many theologians, however, have not been keen on keeping mixed company. Karl Barth and Paul Tillich disagreed about much, but they concurred that theology should pursue its appointed tasks without undue interference from Reimarus, Strauss, Schweitzer and their ilk. To insist on the theological pertinence of con-

2. John Dominic Crossan, *A Long Way from Tipperary: A Memoir* (San Francisco: HarperSanFrancisco, 2000), pp. 150-51.

3. Joachim Jeremias, *Jesus and the Message of the New Testament*, ed. K. C. Hanson (Minneapolis, MN: Fortress, 2002), pp. 1-17.

temporary assertions about the historical Jesus is to make a sort of category mistake. How could proclamation of the gospel or our ultimate concern ever rest securely on the provisional judgments of historical research? So many have asked the question because it is a great question; and judging from the scant attention that multitudes of modern theologians have paid and continue to pay to the ever-growing critical literature on Jesus, the disinterest of Barth and Tillich is nothing unusual. What can the historical Jesus of Athens have to do with the biblical Christ of Jerusalem? Where two or three historians are gathered together, can the biblical Christ be in their midst?

As to who is right in this matter, if anyone is, it is very hard to say; or rather, I find myself on both sides at once. In parts of this book, I attempt to show that the pursuit of the historical Jesus has taught us some important theological lessons. So I cannot dismiss the quest as nothing but a contemporary nuisance, a passing inconvenience. When we add up all the books and articles, the theological sum is not zero, nor is modern historical criticism necessarily a finishing school for apostates.

At the same time, and as I shall now argue in this chapter and the next, some trepidation is warranted. The quest has been, in many respects, profoundly ambiguous, and I imagine that it may always be so; and how one can or whether one should build theologically upon an ever-changing body of diverse opinion is far from manifest.

The Enduring Discord of the Experts

If contemporary theology wants to include the historical Jesus in its discourse, it is up against grave obstacles, because his identity is unclear. More than one historical Jesus resides between today's book covers. We indeed have a plethora of them. There is the Jesus of Tom Wright, a Jewish prophet and almost, it seems, orthodox Christian. There is the Jesus of Marcus Borg, a religious mystic who dispensed perennial wisdom. There is the Jesus of E. P. Sanders, a Jewish eschatological prophet à la Albert Schweitzer. There is the Jesus of John Dominic Crossan, a Galilean but Cynic-like peasant whose vision of an egalitarian kingdom and nonviolent God stood in stark contrast to the power politics of Roman domination. One could go on. To the outsider, theories about Jesus must seem to crisscross each other to create a maze of contradictions. For the portraits, which serve different constituencies in the marketplace, are to large degree not complementary but contradictory.

Which Jesus should baptize our theology? Or does wisdom side with the cynical sentiment of the old Greek philosopher Xenophanes: "All things are matters of opinion"?

The major critical reconstructions of the Nazarene differ so much because their authors return various answers to the central questions of the quest. Why did Jesus go up to Jerusalem? Did he anticipate his own death or even deliberately provoke others to engineer it? If he did sense where things were tending, with what categories did he interpret his imagined future? And did he think of himself as a prophet or as more than John the Baptist and so as more than one who was more than a prophet? What did he mean by the enigmatic circumlocution "the Son of man"? Did he expect God's kingdom to displace, in the immediate future, all the kingdoms of the world, or are the sayings that seemingly attribute such an expectation to him rather products of the church, or should they bear some other meaning?

Some would no doubt protest that I am leaving the wrong impression. Many of my colleagues seem to believe that their chosen field of study is, like the hard sciences, capable of making genuine advances and that in fact much progress has been made. Have we not taken great strides during the last few decades? Do we not, for instance, know a lot more today about first-century Galilee, first-century Aramaic, and first-century Judaism than ever before? Do we not now have a much better sense of how the Gospels evolved than did our exegetical predecessors? And is there not, in fact, much on which the specialists concur?

I do not wish to deny that "Yes" is the right response to these questions — although it remains true that some of the older books are still pretty good while some of the newer books are surprisingly bad: we are not always and uniformly moving onward and upward. And yet a candid observer would surely see little agreement regarding most of the truly interesting and theologically-charged questions. Progress has not touched all subjects equally, and whatever consensus may exist, it remains mostly boring.

Almost everyone in the guild takes for granted that Jesus was a Jew who lived in first-century Palestine, that his parents were named Mary and Joseph, that he taught in parables, that he spoke about God's reign, and that he was crucified in Jerusalem. But, without elaboration, these uncontroversial facts engage us about as deeply as a list of the U.S. Presidents and their dates; and for theological purposes such facts are like a rainbow drained of all color. Most of us instead would like to know exactly what Jesus meant when he proclaimed the kingdom of God, would like to know about his self-conception, would like to know if he was a sort of pacifist on principle, and would like to know what he saw when he gazed into the future.

Yet even if there were some sort of contemporary consensus on these more interesting and important issues, would it not be unwise to build a house of faith upon a recent academic head-count? Famous names rise and fall. Ideas come and go. Today's consensus will be tomorrow's memory. Big books on Jesus are like the clouds: no matter how large, imposing, and beautiful they may be, they never last for long. There will never be any definitive non-canonical edition of his life.

We need some perspective here, which the past supplies. Sixty years ago, an informed British theologian might well have thought it prudent, having read C. H. Dodd, T. W. Manson, and Vincent Taylor, to take their concurrence as a safe court of appeal. Those three New Testament scholars were, at the time, and at least in England, a sort of academic trinity, the big names to be reckoned with; and surely, one might have surmised with some justification, their agreement on a matter constituted the scholarly consensus about it.

Although such would indeed have been the consensus then, nothing lasts. Any theological thinking that turned Dodd, Manson, and Taylor into a collective polestar by which to navigate would have gone off course as soon as those three mortals and their commanding influence passed away. Likewise, any contemporary theology that takes its bearings from contemporary reconstructions of the historical Jesus will be defunct as soon as those reconstructions become defunct, which will not be very long.

We may, out of foolish pride, imagine that our contemporary results will somehow prove to be more important and to have a longer shelf-life than those of our scholarly ancestors; but we will become passé soon enough. Our academic descendants will look back on our writings as we look back on the works of the nineteenth century: maybe a few of our writings will be of antiquarian interest, but any authority they once had will be long gone. This is one reason why I am allergic to the phrase "assured critical result." Those three words — which too often function as a simplification for novices and as an excuse for scholars to think less — fail to resonate with my experience, which is rather that the discourse of New Testament scholars is Heraclitean: everything keeps changing. Working with "assured critical results" reminds me a bit of the old saw about shoveling frogs into a wheelbarrow: they keep coming out even as one is trying to shovel more in.

Study of the historical Jesus belongs to the diversity and pluralism of modernity, or, if you prefer, postmodernity, and there can be no easy appeal to the consensus on much of anything. The biblical guild is not a group-mind thinking the same thoughts. Nor are the experts a single company producing a single product, "history." As Chesterton says somewhere: "There is no history; there are only historians." The unification of academic opinion would be almost as miraculous as the union of the churches. If you are holding your breath waiting for the consensus of the specialists, you will pass out.

So if we are to do something with the historical Jesus, it will have to be someone's particular historical Jesus — Wright's Jesus or Crossan's Jesus or Sanders's Jesus; it can no longer be the Jesus of the guild or the Jesus of the scholars, because they, in their writings and at their academic conferences, argue with each other over almost everything. The Jesus Seminar was not a problem because of its results — anyone knowing the history of the discipline had encountered such before — but because its publicity machine tried to pass off its conclusions as the official consensus of scholarship. The voting in the Seminar, however, represented only one school of thought within the guild, not the guild as a whole, for which no individual or group is the elected representative. And has not the Seminar already ceased to be the latest fashion?

Perhaps, one may suppose, I am being too cynical. That there are persistent differences on the subject of Jesus is not to say anything surprising or profound. There were radically different takes on Jesus from the beginning. From one point of view, one might even say that the quest began before Easter, when people rendered their different verdicts about him. Indeed, Jesus himself, if we can trust the sources, joined in the quest, offering controversial accounts of what he had done and what it meant. "If I by the finger of God cast out demons," Luke has him say, "then the kingdom of God has come upon you" (11:20) Again, two Evangelists have him responding to a question from John the Baptist with these words: "Go and tell John what you hear and see: the blind receive their sight, the lame walk, the lepers are cleansed, the deaf hear, the dead are raised, and the poor have good news brought to them. And blessed is anyone who takes no offense at me" (Matt. 11:4-6; cf. Luke 7:22-23).

Although people have always disagreed about Jesus, many have nonetheless found enough faith to cherish their own opinions about him. I certainly have. Beyond that, if we were to withhold judgment on some issue because informed individuals disagree about it, we would have to give up all knowledge. What academic field of study is not riven by the obstinate disputations of the experts? And what religious opinion is without its countless dissenters? If we were to dismiss the quest just because of its vast range of differing opinions, we would also have to abandon theology, which is scarcely a pleasant hamlet of harmony. If we are to believe anything, we must get used to disagreeing with lots of other people.

Still, one understands the reluctance of Barth and Tillich and so many others to make their theology depend in significant ways on the quest for the historical Jesus and its ever-evolving discourse. "Nobody," Rudolf Bultmann pontificated half a century ago, "doubts that Jesus' conception of the Kingdom of God is an eschatological one — at least in European theology and, as far as I can see, also among American New Testament scholars."[4] Many theologians, weaned with this purported knowledge, naturally felt obliged to come to theological terms with an apocalyptic Jesus who proclaimed the nearness of the end. One thinks, for instance, of Wolfhart Pannenberg, whose well-known book on christology, *Jesus — God and Man,* is largely an exercise in vindicating an eschatological worldview, an exercise set in motion by the conviction that Jesus was an apocalyptic prophet.

A few decades after Bultmann, however, Marcus Borg gave it as his judgment that "the majority of scholars" no longer attributes to Jesus the eschatological view that Bultmann attributed to him: that had, allegedly, become an antiquated position.[5] Borg himself has gone on to do popular Christian theology and to speak to large crowds outside the academy in the conviction that it was Schweitzer, Bultmann, and Pannenberg who

4. Rudolf Bultmann, *Jesus Christ and Mythology* (New York: Charles Scribner's Sons, 1958), p. 13.

5. Marcus J. Borg, *Jesus, A New Vision: Spirit, Culture, and the Life of Discipleship* (San Francisco: HarperSanFrancisco, 1987), p. 14.

were wrong about Jesus, not Jesus who was wrong about the end. Here, then, we have a case in which theology seems to vary with what one takes to be the current academic consensus about Jesus.

Even if one does not find this circumstance disconcerting, there remains the problem of the amateur and the expert. Whereas the quest for the historical Jesus is written up by professionally-trained historians, other individuals with different training typically do our theologizing; and do not the latter revert to amateur status when they leave their area of expertise and survey another subject? Perusing books they could not have written and scrutinizing the conflicting arguments of the recognized specialists, are they not a little like me trying to figure out the brain-mind problem by struggling through a few books of philosophy and neuroscience? What are the odds that I am going to get much right? Likewise, what are the odds that the theologian is going to figure out which historians are the best? There is no referee to declare a winner, only a confusing and interminable game. How, in this era of ever-escalating, esoteric specialization, do the amateurs judge the experts? Whom should we follow through the quest's labyrinth of doubt and speculation?

In my experience, some theologians evade the issue by utilizing what they learned about New Testament studies during their early formal training. Recently I noted that the works of a prominent contemporary theologian frequently refer to the writings of Oscar Cullmann, a one-time giant in the field. Why? My guess is that, when this person attended seminary and then graduate school several decades ago, he had teachers who spoke about Cullmann in class and who assigned their students to read Cullmann outside class. For better or worse, however, New Testament scholars are no longer much reading Cullmann: his day has gone. Yet our theological author, undoubtedly inundated by the flood of literature in his own area of proficiency, almost certainly does not have the time, even if the inclination were present, to sort through more recent contributions from living New Testament scholars. The theologian, then, inevitably ends up using, from the guild's point of view, dated materials. (Sadly, I might add, even the experts cannot keep up any more. The number of publications has become as the sand of the sea. Attending the displays of new books at the annual Society of Biblical Literature meetings produces in me mostly despair, because I know that, amid the myriads of throw-away books, are thousands of valuable pages that I will never turn.)

Theologians are in a sort of quandary as I see it, and I do not know how to help them crawl out of it. They can do one of three things. First, they can rely on their dated knowledge, gleaned during their school days, of what New Testament scholars have written about Jesus. This will guarantee that on some important matters they will be holding judgments that have since been revised or abandoned.

Second, they can attempt to acquaint themselves with contemporary work. In this case, they will manage to sample only some of what is out there, and they will be faced, as just observed, with the arduous task of deciding, as amateurs, which purported authorities are right and which are wrong.

Third, they can simply go on their own way and ignore the quest as a matter of indifference, remaining undisturbed in their theological convictions, hoping or believing that nothing much important has been or is going on, or at least nothing much religiously important. Why cudgel our theological brains with an assemblage of incongruous and theologically arid theories?

This last tempting option is no more commendable than the first two. Not only does it perhaps leave the theologian inadequately prepared to address people sincerely confused by critical study of the Gospels, but who can doubt that the quest has, as a matter of historical record, changed the modern theological landscape? Has it not made many Christians think in new ways about both Jesus and Christian origins? Has it not, for example, made manifest as never before how indebted to intertestamental Judaism are the canonical Gospels and how substantial are the disagreements among them? Has it not raised awkward questions regarding Jesus' self-conception and his eschatological expectations? And what reason can we have for thinking that the quest will not raise additional questions of substance in the future? Even the claim that theology and faith should be independent of historical research is itself a response to the challenges that modern historical criticism has bred. Altogether ignoring the historians does not seem to be any more prudent than hoping to discover in their writings some sort of underpinning for or vindication of one's version of Christian theology.

The Enduring Challenge of Personal Predilection

If the discord of the experts and the difficulty of judging among them are stumbling blocks for theologians wanting to do something with some-body's historical Jesus, equally challenging is the circumstance that no-body's historical Jesus is the product of unsullied historical thinking. All or almost all of the big books on Jesus come with what we may call a built-in theology.

Introductions to the quest of the historical Jesus routinely remark that Albert Schweitzer showed us that many of the critical lives of Jesus written during the nineteenth century were deeply uncritical, at least in-sofar as they were largely projections of the theological views of their au-thors. Such introductions may also quote, as illustration, George Tyrrell's famous remark that Adolf Harnack, "looking back through nineteen cen-turies of Catholic darkness," beheld "only the reflection" of his own "Lib-eral Protestant face, seen at the bottom of a deep well."[6]

One wonders what effect recalling Schweitzer and Tyrrell has on a novice readership. Do some suppose that contemporary scholars have fi-nally learned the lesson and so no longer execute self-portraits and call them "Jesus"? One also wonders about the impression left by those who (without good reason, in my judgment) speak of a third quest for the his-torical Jesus and characterize it by its relative lack of theological agenda. Have we really begun to extricate ourselves from our ideological pas-sions? Do our academic masks hide nothing but academic faces?

Some contributors to the quest have, we may grant, no explicit theo-logical interests, and others do an excellent job of hiding theirs. And speaking for myself, I know, from introspection and from reading John Meier's big books on Jesus, that even a professing Christian can write about the historical Jesus without consciously trying to score theological points at every turn.[7] But ideology, as everyone should know by now, is everywhere nonetheless, and surely a modern Schweitzer would not struggle to espy the myriad ways in which personal predilections have greatly influenced recent investigations of Jesus.

---

6. George Tyrrell, *Christianity at the Cross-Roads* (London: Longmans, Green and Co., 1913), p. 44.

7. John P. Meier, *A Marginal Jew: Rethinking the Historical Jesus* (3 vols.; New York: Doubleday, 1991, 1994, 2001).

Who doubts that authors who themselves have a high christology tend to write books in which the historical Jesus himself has a high christology? Or that those who are uncomfortable with Nicea and Chalcedon more often than not unearth a Jesus who humbled rather than exalted himself? The correlations between personal belief and historical discovery must be endless. Jesus seems friendly to evangelical Protestantism in books written by evangelical Protestants, and he is a faithful Jew in books written by non-Christian Jews who want to reclaim Jesus. It is easy to be suspicious here. You can do anything with statistics, and you can do anything with Jesus, or at least a lot of different things.

It is even possible, I have learned to my dismay, to be cynical about oneself. For some time, I have been fascinated by one form of what the literary critics call "intertextuality," by how a text augments its meaning by deliberately interacting with well-known predecessor texts. My absorption in this subject led me, some time ago, to write a book examining the ways, often very subtle, in which the author of Matthew recalls the story of the exodus and the life of the lawgiver, with the result that his Gospel narrates a new exodus and his Jesus becomes a new Moses.[8]

A few years later, I wrote a book on how the texts common to Matthew and Luke but absent from Mark — the so-called Q material — relate themselves to the Jewish Bible. I argued that those texts are full of the Old Testament, which they quote, echo, rewrite, and argue with. This second book is entitled *The Intertextual Jesus,* and its last chapter attempts to pass from our written texts to Jesus of Nazareth. I end up arguing that the flesh-and-blood Jesus, like his literary namesake in Q, engaged the Jewish Scriptures; that is, the intertextual Jesus of Q is not a misleading representative of the historical Jesus, who creatively linked his speech and his activities to portions of the Old Testament.[9]

It was only some time after my book on Q appeared in print that I opened my eyes to the obvious: I had created a Jesus in my own image, after my own likeness. Having enthusiastically preoccupied myself with the study of intertextuality for a decade, I had happily discovered that the Jesus of ancient Palestine was just like me, at least in one important

---

8. Dale C. Allison, Jr., *The New Moses: A Matthean Typology* (Minneapolis, MN: Fortress, 1993).

9. Dale C. Allison, Jr., *The Intertextual Jesus: Scripture in Q* (Harrisburg, PA: Trinity Press Intl., 2000).

respect. He may have been a first-century Jew and so in many ways a stranger and an enigma, but he was also skilled at setting up the sorts of intertextual dialogues that I love to unravel. So I had found Jesus, and he just happened to be a learned and admirable expositor, a man after my own intertextual heart.

That book has not been the only occasion of my siring a congenial Jesus that looks a bit like me. A couple of years before *The Intertextual Jesus* appeared, I published a book entitled *Jesus of Nazareth: Millenarian Prophet.*[10] In this I argued that Jesus was an apocalyptic prophet whose vision of God's reign remaking the world has yet to be fulfilled. I further argued that Jesus embodied and promoted, at least among his closest followers, a sort of mild asceticism. Now anyone who knows me might well wonder how all this could be in any way a personal projection. I am not looking for the end of the world anytime soon, and my amateurish excursions into asceticism ceased long ago: these days I do not even fast during Lent.

Yet I would be deceiving myself were I to imagine that my Jesus was nothing but the product of brutal historical honesty. I wrote *Jesus of Nazareth* during an exceedingly miserable period in my life. The details are irrelevant. I need only say that my prospects for happiness seemed to have come and gone, and I was sunk in a slough of despond. And — this is the point — my chief consolation was hope for a life beyond this one where things might be better, which means that I was comforted by a historical Jesus who seemed ill at ease in the world as it is, a Jesus who did not expect much good from this present evil age, a Jesus who hoped chiefly in a God of the future. If, at that point in time, my research had instead confronted me with an optimistic Jesus peddling a social program for bettering this world, he would have meant much less to me. In retrospect, an alienated Jesus with a transcendent hope was probably the Jesus I needed at the time.

How does it stand with others?

Let me briefly consider a second individual, the late Robert Funk, the principal organizer of the much-loved and much-hated Jesus Seminar. Funk's theological orientation is manifest from his last book, *Honest to Jesus,* which is wholly candid about "the aim of the quest," which is, to

10. Dale C. Allison, Jr., *Jesus of Nazareth: Millenarian Prophet* (Minneapolis, MN: Fortress, 1998).

Funk's mind, "to set Jesus free."[11] Free him from what? From the ecclesiastical creeds and especially from the beliefs of the conservative churches of North America. Funk turned the historical Jesus into a wrecking ball with which to bash the walls of institutional, creedal Christianity.

Whatever the biographical impulses may have been, Funk was a well-known type — the anti-fundamentalist. With this in mind, it is fascinating to follow him as he strolls with us through the Jesus tradition, pointing out what represents Jesus and what does not. The tradition, it goes without saying, often depicts Jesus as an apocalyptic prophet, and it regularly presents him as speaking about himself in exalted fashion. The tradition further purports that Jesus thought in terms of the saved and the unsaved, and it frequently has him quoting from and alluding to the Bible. Funk's historical Jesus, however, is emancipated from all of this. He has no eschatology to speak of, no christology to speak of, and no soteriology (in the traditional sense) to speak of, and he shows little interest in the Bible. Funk exports to the post-Easter period all the sayings and stories that might indicate otherwise.

Although I may be entirely mistaken in the matter, I cannot but wonder about the relationship between Funk's theological preferences and his historical conclusions. Eschatology, christology, soteriology, and the Bible, while at the heart of American fundamentalism, are no part of Funk's personal theology. Jesus is coming again, the fundamentalist says. Funk denies this. Jesus is Lord, the fundamentalist says. Funk thinks otherwise. Jesus saves, the fundamentalist says. Funk has other roles for Jesus. The Bible tells me so, the fundamentalist says. Funk retorts: Well, maybe it does, but it "is a highly uneven and biased record."[12]

Whereas the fundamentalist cites the Bible, Funk instead appeals to the Jesus he has reconstructed, a Jesus who functions to replace the canonical texts, and who in each instance turns out to be Funk's precursor, not the helpmeet of Funk's religious opponents. Those elements in the tradition most beloved of conservatives conveniently happen to be, without exception, post-Easter fictions. Funk's Jesus is on Funk's side. It seems, a cynic might muse, almost too good to be true.

Now I do not contend here that the utility of Funk's Jesus means that Funk must be wrong about everything (although, as it happens, I heartily

---

11. Funk, *Honest to Jesus*, p. 300.
12. Funk, *Honest to Jesus*, p. 314.

disagree with much that he has to say). His conclusions are offered as the products of arguments, and they merit being met by arguments. They certainly cannot be undone by observations about Funk's biography or personal convictions. Were I to imagine otherwise, fairness would require that I shoot *ad hominem* arrows at my own Jesus on the grounds that an intertextually savvy and otherworldly prophet is suspiciously congenial. Still, the ease with which Funk's historical Jesus comes to Funk's theological assistance inexorably precipitates within me some cynicism.

John Dominic Crossan has worried about this matter of personal predilection a great deal because he has been accused of overlaying his own Irish history onto the Jesus tradition. According to some of his critics, Crossan's "interpretation of Jesus as a first-century Galilean peasant resisting Roman imperial injustice in the name of Jewish tradition" represents the "nineteenth-century Irish peasant resisting British imperial injustice in the name of Catholic (or Celtic) tradition."[13]

In response to this charge, Crossan does not deny that there is, in his mind, an analogy between the ancient Jews and the modern Irish, but he insists — sounding to me a lot like the philosopher Gadamer — that we seek the space between narcissism and positivism, which he labels "interactivism." By this he means we should "attempt to create as honest a dialectic as possible between the past and the present, between the viewed and the viewer."[14]

This seems to me a perfectly reasonable response. Although most of us writing about Jesus have theological interests, we cannot be dismissed as doing nothing more than whittling a peg on which to hang our personal agendas. We necessarily see with our own eyes, and whenever we enter a text we cannot leave ourselves behind: the first person singular we always have with us. We also, however, have the magical ability to be self-aware and so self-critical. Not only can we appreciate that our own perspective and our own prejudices are not shared by all, but we can conduct a self-inventory and query our own motives and presuppositions, as Crossan has done in his autobiography and as I have tried to do here and elsewhere. While we inevitably read ourselves into the texts, we can at the same time come to conclusions that neither arise solely from

13. Crossan, *Long Way,* pp. 150-51.
14. Crossan, *Long Way,* p. 152.

our expectations nor simply confirm our wishes. Furthermore, we are not in this alone but are members of a guild. The predispositions of one jostle against the predispositions of another in a sort of communal dialectic, which enables those who so desire to enlarge themselves.

More than this, our prejudices can, it should go without saying, help as well as hinder. I would argue that Jesus was a deeply religious personality who interpreted everything in terms of an unseen world, and that those who are themselves religious might for that reason alone be in some ways better equipped to fathom him than those of a more secular bent. Being like another can aid understanding. This is why Gentiles have learned much from Jewish scholars about Jesus the Jew.

I have, over the last few pages, tried to make the best of a worrisome situation. To be predisposed is not, I have urged, to be inescapably wrong. A predilection need not always blind us. Sometimes it may instead help us to see more clearly. I also believe that we can, if our vision is obscured, sometimes take the log out of our own eye.

At the end of the day, however, I cannot exorcise all of my concerns about our biased subjectivity. It remains the case that much Jesus research appears captive to ideological predilections in worrisome ways. If we could but peer beneath all the sophisticated arguments, we would find that much of the disparity in our field is not unrelated to intractable differences of philosophical outlook and religious commitment. Professional historians are not bloodless templates passively registering the facts: we actively and imaginatively project. Our rationality cannot be extricated from our sentiments and feelings, our hopes and fears, our hunches and ambitions.

Consider the fact that Funk has labeled Jesus a "secular sage" who was "irreligious, irreverent, and impious."[15] This novel evaluation, which could arise only in the modern academy, is not very shrewd. It is about as compelling as the legend that Jesus died in Kashmir, or the occasional attempt to turn Jesus into a revolutionary zealot bent on taking up the sword against Caesar. I cannot but surmise that an ideological program — Funk's desire to use the historical Jesus against institutionalized religion — has distorted perception here.

Again, to take an example from a more conservative source, consider N. T. Wright's evaluation of the following lines from Matthew's ac-

---

15. Funk, *Honest to Jesus*, p. 302.

count of the crucifixion: "At that moment . . . the earth shook, and the rocks were split. The tombs also were opened, and many bodies of the saints who had fallen asleep were raised. After his resurrection they came out of the tombs and entered the holy city and appeared to many" (27:51-53). This astounding series of prodigies left no trace in the other Gospels or Acts or Paul or, for that matter, Josephus; and if such marvels really had some basis in fact, they would instantly have become the bedrock of Christian apologetics, especially as the text speaks of many graves and many witnesses. But all we have is Matthew's two and a half verses, written sixty or so years after the crucifixion. Surely, then, if anything in the New Testament is haggadic fiction, this is it. Wright, however, has this to say: "some stories are so odd that they may just have happened," and Matt. 27:51-53 "may be one of them." These lame words lack all historical sense. They are pure apologetics, a product of the will to believe, and a prize illustration of theological predispositions moving an intelligent man to render an unintelligent verdict.

As with Funk, so with Wright: the past is not being discovered but avoided. Predilections can strangle truth. There is, moreover, no reason to imagine that Wright and Funk are our most egregious sinners, aberrations in an otherwise less biased, more conscientious society of scholars. Is this fact not disquieting?

The other concern I cannot exorcise is this. If some theologians really care about the historical Jesus, they may sense an ethical imperative to do more than just assemble him out of their own theological predispositions. Yet this presents a problem. Such theologians, for reasons I have indicated, will not be able to use the historical Jesus of the scholars in general, who disagree about so much, but only the Jesus of some particular scholar or school. But how will our theologians go about deciding which school or scholar?

I am not sure what the answer should be in theory, but I am certain that, in practice, the method is that of attraction. Theologian A adopts the reconstruction of historian B because theologian A likes the Jesus of historian B. And the fondness of A for B derives undoubtedly from theological congruency. That is, A and B share similar ideological inclinations. So whereas some theologians may earnestly wish to appeal to the Jesus of history and may think they are in fact doing this, what happens more often than not is that they are really utilizing the Jesus of their own theological predilections, because those are also the predilections of the historian(s) they have chosen to follow. Like is attracted to like. All one need to do to see the truth of the matter is ask, Which pastors and theologians have made use of the Jesus Seminar and which pastors and theologians have made use of Tom Wright?

The Perceptions of Others and Personal Identity

The modern quest for the historical Jesus began with the European deists, who were interested in anti-ecclesiastical readings of the evidence. Operating with a hermeneutic of suspicion long before the advent of that term, they doubted that the church's Jesus was the real Jesus, and they set out to prove this. Their goal was to separate truth from fiction — the truth about Jesus from the fiction of the church. They wanted to erase the tellers from their tales and to find the undisguised identity of the historical individual behind the institutional Superman.

One understands and may even sympathize. Institutions always rewrite the past and mythologize it to their own ends, and the ancient churches cannot have been the one exception to this sociological rule. Religious figures grow in the telling, and memories morph into legends. It makes sense to attempt to disentangle the historical Buddha, if there was one, from all the fabulous stories later wound about him. It makes sense to seek for the historical Muhammad beneath the mountainous tel of Islamic tradition. And it makes sense to distinguish Francis of Assisi from the Francis of fable, whose delightful miracles multiplied as the decades after his death rolled on.

In like fashion, it seems sensible, from the historical point of view, to quest for the pre-Easter Jesus, on the assumption that our sources, like the sources for everybody else who matters, are not innocent of exaggeration and invention. So, we may want to know, what was Jesus like before his pious followers painted over his portrait with their distortions and legends. Can we scrape off the overlay?

I understand the questions and do not reject the enterprise they have generated, an enterprise to which I have tried to contribute. I am keenly interested in the relationship between story and memory, between memory and interpretation, and between interpretation and misinterpretation. I must confess, however, that, with every year of further contemplation, I become more uncertain about anyone's ability, including my own, cleanly to extricate Jesus from his interpreters. Matthew 13 assigns to angels the task of separating the good fish from the bad fish, and I think it may take supernatural talent to go through the net of tradition and throw out what does not come from Jesus.

More importantly, I have become much less sure of exactly what I am trying to accomplish when I look for the treasure of Jesus buried in the field of the church. The problem is that I have come to appreciate the obvious, which is that personal identity cannot be isolated from social identity. Although many of us have imagined that we put the historical Jesus on display by isolating precisely what he said, precisely what he did, and precisely what he thought about himself, no one's identity can be reduced to words or deeds or self-consciousness, or to some combination thereof. Let me explain.

In moments of serious reflection, people sometimes ask themselves, Who am I? It is a perplexing question. It encompasses the past, the present, and the future; it must account for feelings as well as thoughts; and — the point I wish to underline — it sets before the mind's eye the faces of the many people with whom one has had significant interactions. So the question quickly becomes, Who am I in relation to others, and who are they to me? I am reminded of the Russian sociologist Alexander Luria, who reported that when, in the 1930s, he asked an illiterate peasant in Uzbekistan about his character, the answer was: "How can I talk about my character? Ask others; they can tell you about me. I myself can't say anything."[16] Makes sense to me. The one is inseparable from the many. We are all one body. Even the desert anchorite and a so-called mountain man cannot avoid taking along with them to their solitude all that they have learned from others before they left them.

Before returning to Jesus, it may be helpful to ponder for a moment what critical methods we might employ to investigate the identity of some other human being, say the author of this book. Who am I, really? I suppose that you could ask me, but if you stopped there, the picture would be woefully incomplete and distorted, would it not? I might, of course, be full of helpful facts about myself — although I fear that I might, like Davy Crockett, enjoy throwing in a few entertaining whop-

---

16. A. R. Luria, *Cognitive Development: Its Cultural and Social Foundations* (Cambridge, MA/London: Harvard University Press, 1976), p. 149.

pers not wholly tethered to the truth. But I think that one would also want to talk to some other people, say my wife and children. In fact, they must know all sorts of things about me that I do not know or might not think or want to tell others. For the same reason, one would desire to interview siblings and other relatives, life-long friends and current students, participants in the biblical guild and faculty colleagues, members of past churches I have attended and members of the church I now attend. All these informants, it goes without saying, would enrich one's understanding of Dale Allison, of who he has been and who he is today. To suppose instead that one could find the real or the authentic or the original or the historical Allison by disregarding the testimonies of family, friends, and acquaintances in order to focus solely on what I have done or said would be silly.

Maybe, however, we have been a bit silly with regard to the historical Jesus. Maybe we have unthinkingly reduced biography to autobiography. Certainly we have sought to set aside Matthean redaction and Markan theology so that we could get back to Jesus as he was before people wrote him up. But should we not be more circumspect here? Of course people can be misunderstood, and fictions may be told about them. At the same time, fictions need not be misleading. Many of the legends about Francis no doubt catch his character; and although Heraclitus never said exactly, "You cannot step into the same river twice," the aphorism nicely sums up one of his central themes. Beyond that, people can misunderstand themselves or remain oblivious to what others see in them. Even more importantly, they cannot take the measure of their lives as a whole because such becomes apparent only after they have died, perhaps only long after.

Giving up the ghost does not halt the waves of influence emanating from our lives; these continue, after we have gone, to propagate and run into the waves of others, creating new interference patterns. This is why a biography of Abraham Lincoln that confined itself to Lincoln's own words and deeds, a biography wholly lacking the reminiscences and interpretations of others, a biography forbidding admittance of any information subsequent to April 15, 1865, the day of his assassination, would be dissatisfying and riddled with holes. Self-perception is only partial perception, and while the passing of time dims memories, it can also unfold significance.

As with Lincoln, so with Jesus. The Nazarene never lived solely to himself, never resided exclusively within his own skin. He was always interacting with others, and their perceptions of him must constitute part of his identity, as must his post-Easter influence and significance. The method of subtraction, the ubiquitous modus operandi of the quest, aspires to erase everything from the record that comes from others or that comes from after Jesus' death; but will that not leave us with an emaciated figure?

Let me answer my question with some examples of how Jesus is present in places where modern historians typically see only the church.

Although I may be wrong about his, the temptation narratives in Matthew 4 and Luke 4 do not strike me as sober history. For one thing, and as Origen already observed, there is no high place from which one can see the whole world. For another, doubting the historicity of the similar dialogues between rabbis and Satan strikes me as sensible, and turnabout is fair play: Why should I evaluate the Synoptic encounter differently? In any event, I concur with many that our story is the product of a sophisticated Christian scribe who spun a delightful haggadic tale out of Deuteronomy and the Psalms. The Son of God repeats the experience of Israel in the desert, where the people were tempted by hunger and idolatry. Having passed through the waters of a new exodus at his baptism, Jesus enters the desert to suffer a time of testing, his forty days of fasting being analogous to Israel's forty years of wandering.

The Jesus Seminar colored all but a tiny portion of Matt. 4:1-11 and Luke 4:1-13 black, thereby indicating the conclusion that the paragraphs are largely or entirely fictive. I suppose I would have gone along with their vote on this one, had I accepted the invitation to join their deliberations, which I did not. But while a black vote was the end of the story for the Jesus Seminar, it is not for me. For this legend is steeped in memories of Jesus. Was Jesus not a miracle worker, as our story presupposes? Did he not refuse to give authenticating signs, just as he does here? Did he not think of himself as leading a victorious battle against the forces of darkness, for which Matthew 4 and Luke 4 stand as fitting illustration? Did he not have great faith in God, a fact that the dialogue between Jesus and the devil presupposes and expounds? The temptation narrative may not be history as it really was, yet it is full of memory. My judgment is that, taken as a whole, its artistic originator has managed to leave us with a pretty fair impression of Jesus, even if the episode does not contain one word that Jesus spoke or narrate one thing that he did. Memory and legend are not easily disentangled, so when we try to weed out the fictions, will we not be uprooting much else besides?

Mark 15 illustrates the same phenomenon. It opens with Jesus' appearance before Pilate and ends with Jesus' burial by Joseph of Arimathea. Its forty-seven verses are almost devoid of Jesus' speech. He utters only two sentences, both cryptic — "You [Pilate] have said so" in 15:2 and "My God, my God, why have you forsaken me?" in 15:34. The chapter also fails to recount any deeds of Jesus, because he is throughout a passive victim of violence, bound and led away here, stripped and nailed to a cross there. If, then, in our quest for the historical Jesus, we care for little save his words and deeds, Mark 15 would seem almost wholly irrelevant.

Beyond that, furthermore, critical scholars have raised some serious questions about the historicity of what is narrated. It is not just that Mark 15:6 is our sole witness to an annual custom of releasing, in response to popular request, a prisoner during a festival, nor that the darkness attending Jesus' death has its parallels in legends about Adam, Enoch, Romulus, and several Roman rulers. Even more problematic is the luxuriant intertextuality of Mark 15: everything rests upon scriptural subflooring. The chapter borrows repeatedly, for example, from Psalms 22 and 69, and whereas Tertullian and Eusebius found in this the over-ruling hand of Providence, many critical scholars find instead the creative hand of Mark and his predecessors. For Crossan, the passion is "prophecy historicized." It is not remembrance but imagination, with a lot of help from the Scriptures.[17]

But is the cult narrative in Mark 15 really just another stretch of canon for the Jesus Seminar to color 99% black? Is it just ecclesiastical theology in story form? Does the historical Jesus disappear before we get to Mark's last two chapters? I think not. Whatever one makes of the historicity of this or that episode, and whether or not Jesus laconically answered Pilate with "You have said so" or despondently ended his life with "Eloi, Eloi, lama sabachthani," Mark's stark account mirrors, in my judgment, not only Jesus' character but also his expectations.

Concerning his character, do we not have in Mark's passion narrative the same man who speaks to us in the Sermon on the Mount, the enigmatic sage who counsels us not to resist one who is evil, who in-

---

17. John Dominic Crossan, *Who Killed Jesus? Exposing the Roots of Anti-Semitism in the Gospel Story of the Death of Jesus* (San Francisco: HarperSanFrancisco, 1996).

structs us to turn the other cheek? He has no harsh words for his enemies. Being reviled, he reviles not. He does not struggle against his
bonds, nor does he spit at those who spit on him. The man persecuted
for righteousness' sake in Mark 15 is the incarnation of the exhortations
in Matthew's inaugural discourse, which means that, if that discourse
faithfully manifests the spirit of Jesus, as it undoubtedly does, then Mark
15 does the same.

As for the relationship between Mark's account of the crucifixion
and Jesus' own expectations, our Evangelist has constructed a striking
series of correlations between his eschatological discourse, Mark 13, and
the chapters it introduces, 14 as well as 15. 13:24 foretells that the sun will
go dark, and this happens when Jesus is on the cross (15:33). 13:2 prophe-
sies that the temple will be destroyed, whereas its veil is torn apart two
chapters later (15:38). 13:9 foresees that the disciples will be "delivered
up," will appear before Jewish councils, will be beaten, and will stand before governors, all of which happens to Jesus soon enough (14:41, 53-65;
15:1-15). 13:35-36 admonishes the disciples to "watch . . . lest the master
come and find them sleeping," and in Gethsemane, after Jesus tells his
disciples to "watch," he comes and finds them sleeping (14:34-42). These
and other parallels reveal that for Mark the eschatological discourse and
the Passion narrative are of a piece: Jesus' death belongs to eschatology.
His demise either foreshadows the latter days, or it inaugurates them.

Although this is a Markan theological construct, it is to my mind a
descendant of Jesus' own eschatological expectations. For, along with
Schweitzer and Jeremias and others, I believe that Jesus anticipated for
himself a fate akin to that of John the Baptist and that he construed his
imagined fate in terms of Jewish eschatology, whose primary pattern is
tribulation followed by vindication. In other words, Mark's literary pattern, which makes the end of Jesus a sort of end of the world in minia-
ture, is not independent of the influence of Jesus' own theology. Rather,
Jesus' eschatological interpretation of his anticipated fate belongs in the
genealogy of causes behind that pattern. Which is to say: the historical
Jesus can show up even in Markan redaction.

For another example of Jesus being present where modern historians never think to look, let me leave the Gospels entirely and travel to
Paul, to his celebrated psalm of love in 1 Corinthians 13. Although the
words in v. 2, "if I have all faith so as to remove mountains, but do not
have love, I am nothing," may echo Jesus' promise about the omnipo-

tence of faith (Matt. 17:20; 21:21; Mark 11:23), the beautiful chapter is entirely Paul's work; it makes no pretense to derive from Jesus. But derive from Jesus, at least in part, it does. Like the Jesus of the Gospels, Paul makes love the chief virtue (Matt. 5:43-48; 19:19; 22:34-40, etc.). Like the Jesus of the Gospels, he says that matters of the heart trump all outward show (Matt. 6:22-23; 12:33-35; 15:7-20, etc.). Like the Jesus of the Gospels, he calls for patience, kindness, and longsuffering (Matt. 5:21-26, 38-42, 43-48, etc.).

The exposition of love in 1 Corinthians 13 so strongly recalls Jesus' words and behavior in the Gospels, including (as Chrysostom, *Homilies on 1 Corinthians* 33 saw) his conduct in the Passion narratives, that some earlier commentators, when arriving at this chapter, decided that Christ must have been its model, and they even wondered whether the pre-Christian Paul had not, after all, known Jesus of Nazareth, a fantasy for which there is of course no evidence. Nonetheless, given that Paul elsewhere shows at least a passing knowledge of Jesus' teaching and character and that, just two chapters earlier, he links self-renunciation to Jesus' precedent (11:1), surely 1 Corinthians 13 reflects the continuing influence of the latter's spirit of self-sacrificial love. Jesus wrote nothing to the Corinthians, but without him 1 Corinthians 13 would not have been written. The author of *1 Clement,* when rewriting 1 Corinthians 13, naturally thought of the love of "the Master" (49:1-6); and Origen, when commenting on 1 Cor. 13:4-5, fittingly found the verses illustrated in Jesus, and he quoted Phil. 2:6-8 ("he humbled himself").[18]

Paul's ruminations on love, Mark's Passion narrative, and the story of Jesus verbally jousting with the devil illustrate, I should like to suggest, what Crossan has termed (albeit with only modern historians in mind) "interactionism," the mean between the extremes of positivism and narcissism. The New Testament offers us neither the historical Jesus unsullied by Christian interests and beliefs and distortions nor Christian distortions and beliefs and interests unsullied by the historical Jesus. For there was always a dialectic. Although ideology imposed itself everywhere, Jesus was not an inert, amorphous lump, waiting for Christian fingers to give him shape. He was not like poor old Enoch, whose laconic five verses in Genesis (5:18, 21-24) set no bounds to speculation, so that he became, in Jewish and Christian legend, a scribe, a proselyte, a

---

18. Origen, *Homily on 1 Corinthians* 51.

preacher, a judge, a king, and the inventor of sewing: quite a list for someone who probably did not even exist. Jesus, by contrast, was a real person and a real memory, and he became a living tradition that encouraged some construals and discouraged others.

The New Testament is, from one point of view, not so different from the modern books on Jesus, which are always the outcome of give and take between traditions and interpreters. Often no doubt we give too much of ourselves and take too little from Jesus, and sometimes we are unwittingly speaking when we assume we are listening. But, in the idiom of Matthew, Jesus is with us always, and with us to some extent in all (I would contend) but the very worst of our modern reconstructions.

It is the same in the New Testament. That Paul was never made out to be preexistent, never equated with the Logos, and never thought to be one with God the Father tells us something about the Apostle whereas the fact that, on the contrary, all this happened to Jesus tells us something about him. Even in John and its soaring discourses, which contain only scattered remnants of words Jesus uttered, he remains a real presence. John's retrospective christology was possible precisely because Jesus made himself out to be the central figure in God's eschatological scenario, and this stupendous self-perception naturally provoked his followers, during and after his ministry, to speculate about his distinctive identity. So the construal in John remains part of Jesus' *Wirkungsgeschichte,* part of the history of his effects, and therefore part of his identity.

If it is true that the ripples of influence radiating from human beings are central to their identities and that death does not halt them, then what are we doing when, in questing for Jesus, we separate the authentic materials from the inauthentic? Is this not perhaps a crude procedure? Does it not presuppose a stark and uncertain antithesis that needs to be set aside from some new and improved thinking? The question will be all the more pressing of course for anyone who celebrates Easter and believes that Jesus Christ cannot be reduced to a bundle of memories, however influential, who believes rather that his death was not the end of his activities.

If I may, in conclusion, use the language of Paul, Jesus became a life-giving spirit, who moved into the early Christians and their texts, with their memories and their fictions, their speculations and their debates. Jesus' life reached beyond itself, to live on in others. If we ignore them, don't we ignore him?

*   *   *

I have, in this chapter, issued some warnings to those of us who wish to put the historical Jesus of modern scholarship to theological use. The abiding quarrels of the experts, their ideological predilections, and the ill-advised aim of finding an unchurched Jesus are large obstacles in our way. Unfortunately, the next chapter offers more discouraging words: this is not an easy business.

CHAPTER 2

Disputed Questions

*"No text is scripture in itself and as such. People — a given commu-
nity — make a text into scripture, or keep it scripture by treating it
in a certain way."*

WILFRED CANTWELL SMITH

"The normative cannot be transcended by the descriptive."

THOMAS NAGEL

When, in the 1970s, I first began studying theology, a number of
books informed me that Christianity is a historical religion. These
volumes stressed that my faith, unlike that of Hindus and Buddhists, had
grown out of real events. To use the titles of two of those books, "The God
Who Acts" had established "Salvation in History."[1] The implication
seemed to be that Judaism and Christianity were, in their historical nature and claims, unique and so preferable.

My teenage mind, interested in knowing what might be distinctive
about Christianity, went along. It made sense to me that the Bible was
largely an interpretation of the Deity's saving activities in the past. Indeed, and in retrospect, this conviction nudged me toward my chosen
profession, biblical studies; and it was years before I cared much about

---

1. G. Ernest Wright, *The God Who Acts* (London: SCM, 1952); Oscar Cullmann, *Salvation in History* (London: SCM, 1967).

anything other than historical questions. I remember one occasion during graduate school when a guest lecturer spoke eloquently about Mark's literary artistry. I was impatient. Who cares about Mark?, I thought to myself. I want to know about Jesus.

Continued study, however, began to teach me that history is not the epistemological bulwark that I had early on expected it to be. Instead of becoming my security, it turned out to be my insecurity. Not only, I decided, will intelligent scholars perpetually debate the really important and interesting issues, but many of those issues will forever remain contested in my own mind. At some point, moreover, I awakened to the obvious: facts do not dictate their interpretation, nor does history carry its own meaning. Theology comes out of history only after one has read it into history. The past, or rather modern historical reconstructions of the past, cannot, then, be the point of departure for religious faith or theology.

Having come to these realizations, I did not go on to infer that the past is theologically neither here nor there, for it seemed obvious that at least a few Christian beliefs require historical correlates, and that some of those correlates might be subject to critical investigation and revision. For example, the words, "suffered under Pontius Pilate," belong to the Apostles' Creed, and they are straightforward enough. If there was no Jesus of Nazareth who died between the years 26 and 37 AD, when Pilate was prefect of Judea, then something thought to be importantly true would be indisputably false; and while it is wildly unlikely that any evidence will ever call into question "crucified under Pontius Pilate," it is conceivable, at least in theory, that new discoveries could change our mind.

Some modern scholars, furthermore, would say that we have already learned a few things that should amend our theological constructions. In Chapter Four, I will join their company. Before taking their side, however, I wish to address several more preliminary subjects, including this one:

How Much History Does Theology Require?

John Keats's poem "On First Looking into Chapman's Homer" ends with these well-known words:

> Then felt I like some watcher of the skies
> When a new planet swims into his ken;

Or like stout Cortez, when with eagle eyes
He stared at the Pacific — and all his men
Look'd at each other with a wild surmise —
Silent, upon a peak in Darien.

It was Balboa, not Cortez, who discovered the Pacific Ocean. Yet the poem is no worse for the error. As M. H. Abrams wrote, the factual mistake "matters to history but not to poetry."[2] One is reminded of what W. B. Stanford said about Homer's *Odyssey*: "For appreciation of his poem and story it makes little difference whether Ithaca is Thiaki or the Isle of Man or Rhode Island."[3]

What then of the canonical Gospels? They, too, are works of literature. Why should we fret much over how much history is in them? Why cannot the Gospels be like the parables that Jesus told? It is beside the point to ask whether he ever learned of a merchant who sold all that he had to buy a pearl of exceeding value; and when some of the church fathers discussed whether the story of a rich man suffering in Gehenna while a poor man is comforted in Abraham's bosom actually took place, they were wasting their exegetical time.

Should we not live by the golden rule whether Jesus spoke it or not? What difference would it make if we learned that he had been crucified not outside the walls of Jerusalem but outside the walls of Jericho? Maybe, some would say, discussions over the historicity of the Gospels are of little more value than the debates as to whether Shakespeare really wrote the plays attributed to him: some of the arguments against the traditional ascription may intrigue, but what can they have to do with the value of the Shakespearean corpus, whose merits are independent of its authorship? If we can separate art from the artist, why can we not separate the literary Jesus from the historical Jesus?

The question gains impetus from modern study of the Bible, for many of us within the churches have changed our minds about the importance of history for understanding any number of scriptural books. We no longer, for example, look to Genesis if we are seeking to gather

2. M. H. Abrams, "John Keats," in *The Norton Anthology of English Literature*, rev. ed., ed. M. H. Abrams, et al. (2 vols.; New York: W. W. Norton & Co., 1968), 2:504, n. 1.

3. W. B. Stanford, *ΟΜΗΡΟΥ ΟΔΥΣΣΕΙΑ: The Odyssey of Homer* (London: Macmillan, 1958), p. xli.

facts about the cosmological or geological past but rather consult geologists and cosmologists. Similarly, we learn about human origins not by reading the Bible as a handbook of natural science but by acquainting ourselves with what anthropologists and scholars of prehistory have to tell us. Adam and Eve have ceased to be historical individuals and are now purely theological figures. This does not mean, however, that Genesis has ceased to function as Scripture. We have learned how to read the text as theology without reading it as history. We can believe in God as creator and profess the world to be good without worrying about the location of Eden or how it is that a snake could speak.

Recognition of the unhistorical nature of some scriptural texts is hardly a recent innovation, even if moderns have gone further than did any of the ancients. Here is a dispute from the Talmud:

> One of the rabbis was sitting before R. Samuel b. Na'hmeni, and as he expounded he said: "Job never was; he never existed. He is only a parable." He (Samuel) said to him, "Against you the text says, 'There was a man from the land of Uz, whose name was Job'" (Job 1:1). But the other retorted, "If that is so, what of the verse, 'The poor man had nothing except one poor ewe lamb, which he had bought up and nourished' (2 Sam 12:3, Nathan's parable for David)? Is that anything but a parable? This [the Book of Job] is also a parable." (*Baba Batra* 15a)

Rabbi Samuel's antagonist was no doubt correct. Job is not fact. It is fiction — as Theodore of Mopsuestia, the fourth-century church father, also recognized, when he likened the book to Greek tragedy.[4] And Job's fictional nature has nothing to do with the book's value.

Theodore and his rabbinic counterpart were not alone in believing that narratives can have theological meaning without being historical. The famous Cappadocian saint and theologian Gregory of Nyssa was taken aback by the tenth plague in the story of the exodus from Egypt. The death of the firstborn made no ethical sense to him:

> The Egyptian is unjust, and instead of him, his punishment falls upon his newborn child, who on account of his infant age is un-

---

4. Theodore of Mopsuestia, *On Job*.

able to discern what is good and what is not good. . . . If such a one now pays the penalty of his father's evil, where is justice? Where is piety? Where is holiness? Where is Ezekiel who said, "The soul that sins is the one that must die," and again, "The son should not suffer for the sin of the father" (Ezek. 18:20)? How can the history so oppose reason?[5]

Gregory answered his own questions by dissolving the narrative's historicity. Unable to find "the true spiritual meaning" in the literal past, he decided that "the events took place typologically" and that we should come away not with a history lesson but with a spiritual lesson: let us by all means extirpate sin at its inception.[6] Origen, Gregory's theological ancestor, was also troubled by the divine violence in Scripture, and he made similar exegetical moves on a number of occasions.

If violence in Scripture forced Origen and Gregory at times to deny its history without denying its theology, modern critical scholarship gives us additional reason to do the same. We now know that Noah's ark comes from the imagination, not memory: there was no universal flood and there was no ark full of animals. One may indeed doubt that any of the stories in Genesis reflect historical events. Similarly, we no longer know, the experts now inform us, that there was a real live Moses: maybe there was, maybe there was not. And if there was a bona fide Joshua, the biblical account of his activities must, given what the archaeologists currently tell us, often stray far from the facts. And so it goes. Much of what people once took to be history is now known to be, or suspected to be, something else. So if meaning is to stay after history has gone, the former cannot inevitably depend on the latter.

Some have no trouble carrying this thought through much of the Gospels. John Dominic Crossan has written that "Emmaus never happened. Emmaus always happens."[7] By this he means that the story in Luke 24 is symbolic, a "metaphoric condensation of the first years of Christian thought and practice into one parabolic afternoon."[8] The rest of the Easter narratives receive similar treatment from Crossan. His ver-

5. Gregory of Nyssa, *The Life of Moses* 2.91.

6. Gregory of Nyssa, *Life of Moses* 2.92-93.

7. John Dominic Crossan, *The Historical Jesus: The Life of a Mediterranean Jewish Peasant* (San Francisco: HarperSanFrancisco, 1991), p. xiii.

8. Crossan, *Historical Jesus,* p. xiii.

sion of the Christian faith does not require that the concluding chapters of the Gospels report historical events. Belief in the resurrection is not, for Crossan, a conviction about Jesus' molecules, about whether they became miraculously reanimated and left his tomb. Indeed, there was, according to Crossan, no tomb at all: Jesus' lifeless body was probably thrown onto a pile for scavengers.

I do not know whether Crossan would say that his historical researches changed his theological convictions or whether he would instead observe that his theological convictions allowed or encouraged his historical conclusions. Maybe he would say that both were true at once.

Whatever the case may be with Crossan, other Christians understandably find themselves with an altogether different view of things. For them, faith without history, indeed without a lot of history, is dead. Some, for instance, may be confident that confession of the resurrection requires that the tomb was emptied by supernatural means. Arguments that it was not, such as are found in Crossan's writings, can only, for such believers, undermine the Christian faith — just as arguments purporting to show, to the contrary, that the tomb was empty can be construed as evidence for the truth of Christianity. One is reminded of C. S. Lewis, who claimed in retrospect that an important contributing factor to his conversion was the realization that "the evidence for the historicity of the Gospels was really surprisingly good."[9]

When opponents of Christianity have used the historical imperfections of the Gospels as theological defeaters, they too have presumed that the historicity of the biblical texts matters greatly. A 2005 book entitled *God without Religion* makes its case against Christianity by, among other things, raising historical questions about Matthew. Did not Matthew mistranslate Isa. 7:14 ("Behold, a young woman will conceive and bear a son") when he turned the old oracle into a prophecy of Jesus' advent ("Behold, a virgin will conceive and bear a son")? And did the Evangelist not misunderstand the poetic parallelism of Zech. 9:9 ("Lo, your king comes to you . . . riding on an ass, on a colt the foal of an ass") and so turn one donkey into two ("they brought the ass and the colt")? That Matthew "manufactured events in Jesus' life from incompetent translations of the Hebrew Bible" entails that "the image of God portrayed in the

9. C. S. Lewis, *Surprised by Joy: The Shape of My Early Life* (New York: Harcourt, Brace & World, 1955), p. 223.

New Testament is unquestionably fictional."[10] How could we find the truth in an imperfect, historically-conditioned human document? Bad history, bad religion.

One recalls Christian polemicists who have assailed Mormonism in like manner, by contending that its distinctive Scripture, the Book of Mormon, is historically inaccurate. They have observed that it incorporates the textual corruptions of the King James Version of the Bible and that its picture of ancient North American civilization does not fit the archaeological record. Thus, they infer, the Book of Mormon cannot be a heavenly tome revealed to Joseph Smith by the angel Moroni. Once again we find the same presupposition: if the history is wrong, the theology cannot be right.

The Roman Catholic Church has officially operated with this same conviction, as the historical-critical fate of Saint Catherine of Alexandria illustrates. According to tradition, the beautiful Catherine denounced the Emperor Maxentius and defeated fifty pagan philosophers in debate. Those philosophers thereupon converted and were consequently burned alive. Catherine herself was thrown into prison, where she was fed by a dove. When her Roman jailers tried to break her on the wheel, it splintered, freeing her and impaling them. She was then beheaded, but her wound poured forth milk instead of blood. Catherine's feast day used to be November 25. A few decades ago, however, she exited the Roman Catholic calendar, for the experts in hagiography decided that her story originated as an edifying romance. Her imprisonment and martyrdom are fictional, it was decided, because Catherine herself was a fiction: she never existed. The church is officially trying to forget her.

Although Jesus is in no danger of suffering Catherine's fate as an unhistorical myth, one may well ask, How much do Christians need to know about him?

Rudolf Bultmann thought that believers need say only that Jesus of Nazareth lived and was crucified. The biblical inerrantist, on the contrary, insists that Jesus must have spoken every word the Gospels attribute to him and done every deed they assign to him, and must have been born of a virgin to boot.

In trying to locate ourselves between these two extremes, the rest of

---

10. Sankara Saranam, *God without Religion: Questioning Centuries of Accepted Truths* (East Ellijay, GA: The Parnayama Institute, 2005), p. 16.

us might entertain the possibility that exegesis can come to our assistance. Why not follow the intention of the texts? When we say that Job is a work of fiction, we may be going against much of the tradition, but we are almost certainly recovering the original intention of the book's contributors. Likewise, maybe historians can show us which episodes the Evangelists thought of as sober history and which they thought of as haggadah, as edifying fiction. Can historical criticism not divine, for instance, that Matthew created the story of Peter walking on the water and intended it to be not history but parable? Can we not also figure out that whoever crafted Matthew's infancy narrative did so out of scriptural materials and knew himself to be fabricating theological parables, not sober history?

There are two problems here. One is that it is, unfortunately, impossible to answer such questions with any real conviction. I have been trying to do it for years and have come up empty. We may not believe that Peter walked on the water, but we have no way of knowing what Matthew thought about the matter. We may also surmise that Matthew's infancy narrative is in part or whole legendary, but I do not see how to determine whether Matthew was of the same mind. There are just not enough clues in his text with which to resolve such issues.

More importantly, the intention of the texts cannot be our sole or even chief guide. Contemporary Christians who read Genesis as theological saga instead of historical record do so not because of what a close reading of the book has taught them but because of what science and archaeology have demanded. That is, convictions acquired independently of the text have moved us to construe it in a certain fashion. And this is the rule for all of our reading: presuppositions extrinsic to the texts govern how we interpret them.

Let me illustrate by briefly turning from history to eschatology. Mark 13:26 pledges that the Son of man will someday come on the clouds of heaven. Determining what that verse meant in the first century is one thing; determining what it means for us today is quite another.

Imagine four different readers: a fundamentalist, a liberal Protestant, a sympathetic non-Christian, and an unsympathetic non-Christian. All four, let us say, agree that the Evangelist Mark expected someday to look up into the sky and to see Jesus riding the clouds. After that, agreement fails. The fundamentalist claims that Mark's literal understanding is binding for interpretation: we, too, should look to the skies, from whence Jesus our Savior will someday return. Our liberal Protestant responds that, whatever the ancients thought, people cannot ride on clouds, so we are compelled to view Mark 13:26 as a mythological statement: the verse is a way of affirming that the God of Jesus Christ will set things right in the end. The sympathetic non-Christian, disbelieving in a deity, disagrees with both the fundamentalist and the liberal and instead finds the real meaning of Mark 13:26 to lie in the fact that people always need hope, even if it is only hope in a myth. The unsympathetic non-Christian then retorts that Jesus has not returned and will never return, and so the true meaning of Mark 13:26 is that Christians are deluded, their faith vain.

The lesson to draw from our four exegetes is that a text is never the sole determinant of its interpretation or application. Readings are rather joint productions; they require not only judgment as to what a text meant to those in the past but also judgment as to what it should or can mean in the present, and the latter involves convictions extrinsic to the texts themselves.

Matters are not otherwise with historical questions: they are observer-dependent and reflect internalized metaphysical and historical assumptions. Determining whether Matthew, Mark, Luke, or John believed something is not necessarily the same as determining whether we can or should believe it. Additional factors are involved, including one's historical sagacity and/or (as with a miracle) one's philosophical disposition and/or (as with Gregory of Nyssa and the tenth plague) one's moral sense. So the question How much history does theology require? has as its answer: It depends on one's presuppositions, one's worldview, one's theology, and so on.

Although this outcome is disappointingly obvious, three attendant considerations keep it from being barren. First, one's theology, worldview, and presuppositions need not be fixed for life, as though a person raised in a particular ideological camp or tradition must be stuck there forever. It is possible, as many of us know from personal experience, to learn to be self-critical and to change one's mind, even on matters of great existential import. Honest reflection can alter perception.

Second, as I have stressed in the preceding pages, many biblical texts that were once presumed to be historical and yet are now known to be unhistorical — Genesis 1, for instance — are still capable of producing theological and religious meaning. This should make all except the fundamentalist cautious about insisting too strongly that authentic Christian faith requires this or that event to be historical. Some things once thought essential and immutable have shown themselves to be inessential and mutable.

Over the past two centuries, more and more of us have learned to get along with less and less history, and who can foresee where the process will or should stop? Does the future hold more of the same? I do not know. But the subject is all the more vexing for me in the light of my students' exegetical papers. When I ask them to write on a passage in the Gospels, I often require that, near the beginning, they address the matter of origin. Does their selected text go back to a word or activity of Jesus? Or did the early Christians rather invent it? How much can be attributed to the Evangelist's hand? I have discovered over the years that the students' decisions about origin, whether well-considered or not, have little or nothing to do with their subsequent exegesis. Their theological, homiletic, and devotional meditations are not organically related to their verdicts about what really happened. The different subjects, to the contrary, remain unconnected. I am left wondering how they can or if they should be connected.

Third, if we can ask How much history does theology require? we can equally ask How much history can historians establish? That is, we can inquire about supply rather than demand. In fact from one point of view one might say it does not really matter what theology wants or thinks that it requires, because this begs the question of what there is to be had. In any event, the subject of what we can expect to get from historians will be the business of later pages. But before turning to that subject, two more questions need to be addressed, the first being:

How Should We Treat Our Texts?

Before the Enlightenment, the canonical Gospels were thought of as, among other things, written copies of the past. The documents and the history beneath them were taken to be, for all practical Christian purposes, identical. Modernity, however, has inserted a wedge between the literary Jesus and the historical Jesus, and it has pried them apart. The experts may not, when dealing with this saying or that event, concur on the degree of distance between the words on the biblical page and what really happened, but no one who is informed can, without further ado, equate the text with the past: the former often strays from the latter. The order of episodes in Luke is not the same as that in Matthew, so at least one of those Gospels does not narrate events according to their historical sequence. And the Jesus of John does not much sound like the Jesus of Mark, so at least one of those representations must be farther from the historical Jesus than the other.

What are we to think when our modern historical reconstructions do not match the narratives of our sacred texts? Does history become our authority and so trump the text? Can history somehow replace the text? And what is the theological status of a passage whose historicity is debated or denied?

Some have no difficulty answering such questions. When text and history depart, defrock the former and coronate the latter. If historical results contradict the claims of a text, then so much the worse for the text: those results rob it of its theological authority.

Such thinking seems almost instinctive to some moderns, who often assume that history can add and subtract from theological authority. Public lectures on archaeology and the Bible often draw large crowds. Perhaps some attendees are genuine antiquarians. Others are probably hoping to find historical props for their biblical faith. Although they may profess Scripture to be authoritative, they nonetheless want it buoyed up by the authority of facts dug from the ground.

What should happen, however, when it is not buoyed up?

Several years ago, the Common Lectionary reading for Sunday included Luke 16:18: "Anyone who divorces his wife and marries another commits adultery, and whoever marries a woman divorced from her husband commits adultery." I know of a Presbyterian pastor who, much taken with the Jesus Seminar, checked the status of Luke 16:18 in *The Five Gospels,* the Seminar's official public statement of its voting results. As it turned out, Luke 16:18 is colored gray, which means that Jesus, in the questionable collective judgment of the Seminar, probably did not utter it. The pastor made this circumstance the excuse for not wrestling with Luke's difficult imperative. Jesus, he told his congregation, was probably not the author of this saying. It was rather formulated by an anonymous early Christian. And why, it was implied, should anyone heed an unknown tradent? Christians, after all, follow Jesus.

Whatever view one takes of divorce or of the origin of Luke 16:18, it must be conceded that this Presbyterian pastor's approach to Scripture could never have occurred to Origen or Augustine, to Calvin or Wesley. The hermeneutical move is distinctly modern — and, in my judgment, clearly mistaken. If only the sayings that Jesus really spoke impinge on us, does this not imply that John's Gospel, whose discourses are so widely thought to be mostly post-Easter meditations, must lose its canonical status altogether?

We also have to ask, if we are to preach only the historical Jesus, whether we should still base sermons on Paul's epistles, for his theology is much more than a reiteration of things that Jesus said and did. Indeed, his theology and practice are in many respects strikingly different from what Jesus said and did. So how can Paul be in any way normative? If, however, we decide that Paul is nonetheless somehow normative, should we not, if we adhere to our pastor's logic, confine ourselves to the authentic Pauline letters? Ephesians and the Pastorals are after all probably pseudepigraphical, and why would anyone refuse to preach on a word dubiously ascribed to Jesus yet preach on a word dubiously ascribed to Paul? What, moreover, should those of us who cannot decide whether Paul wrote Colossians do when a passage from that epistle shows up in the lectionary? Should we expound the text or not? Above all, what happens to the Bible as a whole if history and authorship become criteria for determining theological authority? What, for instance, should we do with the so-called "historical books" of the Old Testament, which contain so much that is not history? And what should we do with paragraphs and chapters that come to us under the name of Isaiah or some other prophet but which, according to critical scholarship, were instead produced by persons forever unknown?

Buddhist eschatology, just like Jewish and Christian eschatology, has it that in the latter days things will go from bad to worse. One old prophecy warns that, among the horrors of the end, the sacred writings will disappear. It is not that the books themselves will cease to exist but rather that their letters will evaporate: the characters will simply vanish from the pages so that the hallowed words will be no more. People will have to face the fearsome end without the guidance of their fortifying Scriptures.

I have sometimes thought of this arresting prophecy when ruminating on our Christian Bible. Although our letters are still on the page, much of the history that we once assumed to be there has in fact evaporated. Not entirely, to be sure. But if we have had a decent religious education, we certainly have less history than we used to; and is it not ironic that it is precisely in this age of diminishing historical returns that so many proceed as though the theological truth of the Gospels depends on the results of historical-critical analysis?

Those who urge that Christian theology should eschew all fiction when constructing its Jesus will have to dismantle Matthew, Mark, Luke, and John, pull out the component parts deemed historical, and put them together in a new way. They will then presumably put their faith in the new reconstruction instead of in the canonical Gospels, in the same way that one might put more trust in a modern book on the Roman Empire than in Suetonius.

Yet this would be to confuse the historical task with the theological task. The status and function of a canonical text within the church are not the same as the status and function of that text within the academy. As a historian, I am all for tearing up the surface of the Gospels and doing the messy work of excavating them for history. As a churchgoer, however, I believe that the Gospels should be preached and interpreted as they stand, as canonical literature. I am persuaded that, for most theological purposes, we should treat the Gospels the same way we treat Genesis; we should use them first of all not to reconstruct the past but to construe our world theologically. Matthew, Mark, Luke, and John are, for the churches, theological texts before they are historical texts.

Maybe here the instinct of my students, when they write their exegetical papers, is sound. As already observed, they typically spend time trying to determine the origin of whatever passage it is they are interpreting. Yet their exegesis rarely if ever hinges on their understanding of a text's tradition history, or even on their verdict, if they can reach one, as to the originating author. My seminarians proceed as if reconstructing the past is one task and expounding the meaning of a text for the present quite another.

The insignificance, at least for certain purposes, of the issue of historicity also becomes apparent when we consider how modern churches have treated John 7:53–8:11, the story of Jesus' encounter with a woman caught in adultery. These verses, which contain several words and constructions found nowhere else in John, are missing from most of the older Greek manuscripts. They are also absent from many Latin, Coptic, Syriac, and Armenian witnesses. Some old manuscripts mark the paragraph with asterisks; others place the lines after John 7:36 or 21:25 or Luke 21:38 or 24:53. For these and other reasons, we know that John 7:53–8:11 was no original part of the Fourth Gospel. Where it comes from, no one knows. And whether it holds a memory of a historical encounter between Jesus and an unfortunate woman, no one knows.

Yet this scarcely makes any difference for practical ecclesiastical purposes. The passage is still in our Bibles and will remain there indefinitely — even if set apart by extra spaces before and after — because the churches have collectively judged it to be memorable and edifying. It matters not that it is a secondary addition (although surely it would if the text were not so edifying: I think then we would cut it out). And it matters not that it may fail to reflect an event in the life of Jesus. What counts is that the text has spoken and continues to speak meaningfully to those in the churches.

It should be the same with the canonical Gospels in their entirety. It is the biblical texts, not the reconstructed history behind them, that have nurtured Christians through the centuries, supplied us with our liturgical readings, been the inspiration for countless sermons, and contributed to Christian doctrine and moral teaching. For theologians or preachers effectively to ignore those portions of the Gospels that some contemporary historians deem unhistorical is to change the rules of the game. It is too late for that. Matthew and Luke may have swallowed up the Sayings Source Q, but Matthew and Luke are not going to be swallowed up. The canon, for better and for worse, has long since been established. Christians cannot abandon it without abandoning their religion. However much they may argue with the Gospels, the Gospels remain the church's heritage and an inescapable part of Christian identity. Believers may need to correct and to reinterpret our Scriptures, but we cannot just jettison them, or parts of them, without ceasing to be ourselves.

Some would loudly protest that jettisoning the Bible, or vast swaths of it, is exactly what Christians need to do, given modern knowledge. Once text and history have split asunder, one cannot hold fast to both; and it is to history that we owe our allegiance.

But one can and we ought to hold fast to both. Nothing compels us to concur with the fundamentalists in insisting — along with, ironically, anti-ecclesiastical polemicists — that, if Jesus and Peter did not literally walk upon the waves, then Matt. 14:22-33 signifies nothing. Such a pettifogging hermeneutical move is unsophisticated and unimaginative, and we should reject it. The texts remain what they have always been, regardless of current views as to the history behind them. Modern historical methods may help us interpret our texts, but they should not depose them. Historical studies of the Bible belong not on the lectern but on the shelves. They are, for the churches, commentaries. Their function is not to displace the canonical texts but to help us better understand them.

Having said all this, let me emphasize that historical reconstructions of Jesus still matter theologically.

Even when theologians no longer view Genesis as a sourcebook of history and science, they must, for certain purposes, still concern themselves with the origins of the cosmos and the origins of the human species. Scientific and historical questions about what really happened remain important, even theologically important, despite the modern verdict that Genesis addresses other issues.

The Gospels and the historical Jesus are maybe not so different. Even as we recognize that the canonical texts cannot be exchanged for the history behind them, this scarcely entails that such history is theologically of no account. Before, however, seeking to show some of the ways in which history is important, I should like to ask another question:

How Might One Come to Know Jesus?

There is more than one Jesus. There is the textual Jesus of antiquity, that is, the several canonical and extra-canonical presentations of him. There is the earthly Jesus of the first century, the man who spoke with Peter and Judas. There is the so-called historical Jesus, or rather the competing modern reconstructions of him. There is the Jesus of church history and tradition, or rather the numerous religious conceptions of him through the ages. And then there is Jesus as he is now, in his postmortem existence, the risen Christ, whom many claim still to encounter, in any number of ways. Jesus is not one but many.

The diversity of images, claims, and experiences poses not only an ontological problem — Who exactly was/is Jesus? — but further an epistemological question: How do we come to know him?

A few things are clear. We become acquainted with the textual Jesus by reading or hearing old books. We cannot, barring invention of a time machine, acquaint ourselves with the earthly Jesus, the son of Mary and

Joseph who lived in Nazareth. We can learn about him only indirectly, through historical reconstruction. Doing history is also how we come to know the Jesus of ecclesiastical tradition: books and articles on Christian doctrine and practice tutor us. As for how one comes to know the risen or contemporary Jesus, this happens through a Christian community, through its worship services, educational programs, and common religious life. Some would add that knowledge of him stems above all from personal encounter, such as feeling his presence or sensing him in one's heart, or even beholding him in a vision.

Our problem is that the various means do not run to the same end. We have John vs. the Synoptics, Athanasius vs. Arius, Wright vs. Borg, and on and on it goes. Our sundry authorities and divers experiences have created a catena of Christs. Who then, among the rivals, is the real Jesus?

Mark's Gospel has Jesus himself already posing this question. Peter returns a succinct answer: "You are the Christ" (8:27-29). I cannot be so laconic. I will instead, in the remainder of this book, introduce several lines of thought that might inform reflection on the vexed subject of Jesus' identity. I begin with the following three points, which I can introduce only briefly:

(1) It is, if we are candid, easy to despair and adopt the indifference of Sherlock Holmes: "Each may form his own hypothesis upon the present evidence, and yours is as likely to be correct as mine." Jesus seems to be a chameleon; he takes his color from whoever re-creates him. Like Odysseus in the first line of the *Odyssey*, he is πολύτροπος, a "man of many turns," of remarkable versatility, who appears now like this, now like that.

We may, however, find some consolation in this, that Jesus, insofar as the representations of him make for a confusing assortment, is not wholly different from the rest of us. We all play several roles in life, and different people perceive us differently. What our immediate families think about us is not the same as what our friends think; and our enemies, if we have any, imagine something else again. It is, moreover, the fate of the famous to be especially subject to multiple and contradictory assessments. If perception is relative, then the more perceivers there are, the more perceptions there will be, and the greater their variety. A wide range of opinions accordingly attaches to all well-known figures, whether they be politicians, entertainers, or religious leaders. Alexander of Macedon, Constantine the Great, and Teresa of Avila have all sat for many dissimilar portraits, as have Martin Luther, Abraham Lincoln, and Queen Victoria. One might, in fact, formulate a rule: the more important people are thought to be, the more diverse the array of verdicts about them. Given Jesus' importance to world civilization and religion, a bewildering mixture of judgments cannot but be expected. Jesus the secular sage vs. Jesus the eschatological prophet vs. Jesus the social reformer, etc., is not so much different than Paul the rabbi vs. Paul the Hellenizer vs. Paul the apocalyptist, etc.

The relativity of perception is, incidentally, hardly a modern discovery. Several ancient Christian texts are familiar with the notion of the "polymorphous Christ." Origen wrote that, although Jesus was a single individual, people perceived him according to their abilities, according to their aptitude and inclination, and so he did not look the same to all, including believers. This idea takes story form in a number of old books, in which Jesus literally looks like John the Baptist to one, like Paul to another, like a woman to another, like a star to another, and like a child to another.[11] One text even declares that Jesus is beautiful and ugly, young and old, great and small, for we all see as capacity permits (*Acts of Peter* 20). It may be that one function of the canon is to set some limits to diversity, so that we do not descend into solipsistic eisegesis; yet it remains true that the nature and identity of Jesus, like the nature and identity of everyone else, are in the eye of the beholder.

What we see is always a function of our being. Adults see things differently than do children, and bats perceive the world differently than do flies. Such physiological and psychological facts have their analogies in the religious realm. Matt. 5:8 says that the pure in heart will see God. This assertion correlates sacred knowledge with one's moral disposition. Knowledge of Jesus has a similar correlation. For Jesus was, among other things, a moral teacher, and the truth of his teaching is in the living. Those who seek to conduct their lives in the light of the canonical accounts of his life and speech will understand him differently than those who find guidance elsewhere. To read a parable that commends feeding the hungry and visiting prisoners is one thing; to respond by visiting

---

11. Origen, *Contra Celsum* 2.64. For Jesus looking like John the Baptist see *Acts of John* 87. For Jesus looking like Paul see *Acts of Paul* 21. For Jesus looking like a woman see Epiphanius, *Heresies*. 49.1. For Jesus looking like a star see the Syriac *Revelation of the Magi* 4.7. For Jesus looking like a child see *Acts of Peter* 21.

prisoners and feeding the hungry is quite another. It is perhaps a bit like being a Shakespearean actor, who experiences a play in ways remote from those of us who never walk the stage. The Sermon on the Mount does not look the same from the outside as it does from the inside.

In this connection I recall the famed words with which Schweitzer ended his *Quest of the Historical Jesus:*

> He comes to us as one unknown, without a name, as of old, by the lakeside, he came to those men who did not know who he was. He says the same words, "Follow me!" and sets us to those tasks which he must fulfil in our time. He commands. And to those who hearken to him, whether wise or unwise, he will reveal himself in the peace, the labours, the conflicts, and the suffering that they may experience in his fellowship, and as an ineffable mystery they will learn who he is.[12]

Although Schweitzer set out to find Jesus through historical-critical sleuthing, and although he believed that he had indeed found him, he also recognized the limitations of his higher-critical tactics and conclusions. He understood that there is, in addition to all our inferences about the history behind texts, the firsthand experience of heeding and following Jesus, of personally striving, as best we can, to enter into his moral and religious vision. Without such effort, our knowledge of him is the less. As the Jesus of Matt. 11:29 says, "Take my yoke upon you, and learn of me."

(2) Countless Christians throughout the ages have said that they know Jesus not just through the memories of the ecclesia or through observance of his words but also through personal encounters with him. What should we say to this?

Let me approach the question by recounting the dramatic vision of a friend of mine. Several years ago she was suffering a personal crisis. Her family life was in trouble, and she was wracked with guilt, indeed felt that she was deserving of hell. One afternoon, while sitting alone in her living room, one of the walls split open, revealing another reality, what appeared to be outer space, with spinning planets and glorious colors she

---

12. Albert Schweitzer, *The Quest of the Historical Jesus,* first complete edition (Minneapolis: Fortress, 2000), p. 487.

had never seen before. Then, amid the planets, she saw a figure walking toward her. Somehow, she knew it was Jesus, although she saw no face. Because of her shame, my friend dropped her eyes to the floor, fearfully awaiting words of condemnation. But her Jesus instead sat beside her and said, "What can I do for you?" She told him, and he responded with encouragement and instruction. Then the living room wall reappeared and everything returned to normal. But my friend was no longer the person she had been before. She felt forgiven, comforted, guided, and she thankfully entered a new and better chapter in her life.

Often our initial response to a report such as this one is to offer an explanation. Either we are credulous, or we are incredulous. We suppose either that Jesus really did appear and speak, or we assert that visions are hallucinations, nothing but projected subjectivity.

The truth to my mind, however, is that, unless we are dogmatic, flat-earth materialists, we cannot be confident as to what actually took place. Because I have myself ostensibly both seen and heard from a deceased friend, and because members of my immediate family and some close friends I trust have had similar experiences, my mind is open to possibilities more than mundane. Regarding visions of Jesus in particular, my thinking is this: if the dead on occasion somehow communicate with the living, as I am inclined to suppose, why should Jesus be incapable of such? At the same time, there is a large body of critical literature on hallucinations, which scarcely encourages us to be naive about them. People, including perfectly normal people, often see and hear things that are not there. Skepticism stands on a solid mountain of evidence.

So I do not claim to know what really happened to my friend in her living room. Maybe she met Jesus, or maybe she beheld a projection of her imagination. But just as we can contemplate the meaning of a saying attributed to Jesus without knowing whether or not he authored it, so too can we contemplate the theological content of visionary and other subjective religious experiences without knowing their etiology.

Whatever the scientific or paranormal explanation of my friend's vision, we recognize her Jesus. He is the canonical Jesus, who acts with compassion and offers forgiveness to those burdened by past failure. He is particularly like the Jesus of John 7:53–8:11, who does not condemn the woman caught in adultery but protects her from others and then encourages her to believe that she can begin her life anew. Indeed, one could plausibly regard my friend's experience as a creative and personal exegesis of certain New Testament texts or stories about Jesus (even if she had not been going to church for twenty-five years).

Perhaps religious experiences that are perceived as encounters with Jesus belong to what the Germans call his *Wirkungsgeschichte,* or "history of effects," and so, as I argued in Chapter One, say something about his identity. For whatever else they may be, christological experiences are responses to biblical and ecclesiastical traditions about Jesus, to the powerful images and ideas Christians have passed down regarding him, ideas and images often much influenced by the canonical Gospels and so (in my judgment at least) partly informed by real memories of Jesus.

This is true not just of the sort of dramatic vision my friend had. It also holds for more run-of-the-mill events. Those who, in a Christian context, feel themselves to be unexpectedly and graciously forgiven are experiencing Jesus' continuing influence. And those who, after reading the Gospels, feel compelled to serve the marginal are responding to his enduring demands.

(3) Matt. 25:31-46, in depicting the last judgment, refers to people who have met Jesus without knowing it. These are the first few verses:

> When the Son of man comes in his glory, and all the angels with him, then he will sit on the throne of his glory. And all the nations will be gathered before him, and he will separate them from each other, as the shepherd separates the sheep from the goats; and he will put the sheep at his right hand and the goats at his left. Then the king will say to those at his right hand, "Come, you that are blessed by my Father, inherit the kingdom prepared for you from the foundation of the world. For I was hungry and you gave me food. I was thirsty and you gave me something to drink. I was a stranger and you welcomed me. I was naked and you gave me clothing. I was sick and you took care of me. I was in prison and you visited me."

This is not the place to argue about the interpretation of a text. I will simply give it as my opinion that "all the nations" includes all of humanity, Christian and otherwise, and that the needy are all in distress, Christian and otherwise. This passage, then, like Jesus' injunction to love even enemies, blurs distinctions between insiders and outsiders. The upshot is that, in this remarkable version of the great assize, religious affiliation or confession plays no role. Deeds of loving-kindness trump everything else — just as they do in the passage where love is the unmatched imperative (Mark 12:28-34) — and salvation is not restricted to those who have entered the ecclesiastical ark. Matt. 25:31-46 is in harmony with the *Apocalypse of Sedrach,* a Christian work of uncertain date which declares that people outside the church can have God's Spirit and on death may enter "the bosom of Abraham."

The interesting point for us is that, in Matthew 25, the doers of good deeds encounter Jesus without knowing it. Although one guesses that Prov. 19:17 ("Whoever is kind to the poor lends to the Lord, and will be repaid in full") is in the background, the precise thought remains opaque. Is the Son of man, who elsewhere in Matthew seems to be the ubiquitous divine presence (18:20; 28:20), somehow mystically united with those who suffer? Or is the connection more formal, so that the world's king, by a sort of royal proxy, identifies himself with his people? Or is some other idea in mind?

Whatever the answer, Christian tradition sometimes attests the notion that one can encounter the divine reality revealed in Jesus of Nazareth without knowing anything about him. The second-century Christian apologist Justin Martyr, rewriting ideas he learned from the Stoics, urged that Jesus was the Word or Logos, "of whom every tribe of men and women partakes," and that "those who [before Jesus came] lived their lives with the Logos were Christians, even if they were reckoned to be atheists, such as, among the Greeks, Socrates, Heraclitus, and those like them" (*1 Apology* 46). Justin also affirmed that the Stoics owed their admirable moral teaching to the "seed of the Logos" planted in them (*2 Apology* 8) and that other pre-Christians spoke well in proportion to the share or part they had in the "seminal divine Logos" (*2 Apology* 13). For Justin, Jesus Christ was the personification of a divine life that had made itself known, to lesser degree, at other times and places.

Justin believed not only that the pre-incarnate Word had spoken to some of the Greek philosophers but also that he had appeared to saints in Old Testament times. According to the apologist, the appearances of "the angel of the Lord" in the Books of Moses were revelations of the Logos (*Dialogue with Trypho* 55-60, 127). Here the notion that some have "entertained angels unawares" (Heb. 13:2) turns into the notion that some have entertained the Son of God unawares, and once more the divine Word active in Jesus of Nazareth is thought of as having been present in the world long before the first century. The idea becomes a picture in Rublev's famous icon of the Trinity, in which Abraham's three angelic visitors are the three persons of the Godhead.

Whatever one makes of Justin's exegesis of Old Testament theophanies or of his philosophical conception of the Logos, Christian theology has always sought to enlarge the person of Jesus. The doctrines of his preexistence and of his session at God's right hand are ways of saying that his birth to Mary and Joseph was not his beginning and that his death on a cross was not his end. The cosmic christology of Colossians 1 holds the same message. The divine reality incarnate in Jesus cannot be confined to one man's span of life; rather, the activities of the Logos contain but exceed the activities of a first-century human being. Those who think like this may well wonder, as did Justin Martyr, whether or how that divinity might be revealed to people unacquainted with the Christian traditions about Jesus.

I will not pursue further this line of inquiry, which is inevitably speculative. I simply observe that, for those with certain religious convictions, the divinity manifested in Jesus of Nazareth cannot be reduced to that historical figure, so the question of how people might come to know that divinity is all the more complicated.

CHAPTER 3

How to Proceed

"I have failed a good many times. My authority is therefore practical ... like that of some ... statesman or social thinker dealing with Unemployment or the Housing Problem."

G. K. CHESTERTON

"I have found it difficult to remember the precise words used in the speeches which I listened to myself, and my various informants have experienced the same difficulty."

THUCYDIDES

"Only the general impression of the words of Jesus can be used."

FRIEDRICH LOOFS

I often attend professional meetings, a circumstance that allows me to speak face-to-face with academics engaged in the current quest of the historical Jesus. A number of them are earnestly enthusiastic about the present moment. The contemporary study of Jesus is, they insist, new and improved; and the so-called third quest, having remade our tool kit, has manufactured better products. Like physicists and biologists, we have seen genuine advances in our knowledge. And maybe, if everyone would just summon the good sense to follow the proper methodology, we would at last come to an authentic consensus on the important questions. What better time to be alive, if one wants to learn about the historical Jesus?

In my youth, when I was more ardent and innocent, I might have been carried away by the enthusiasm of some of my colleagues. No longer. Now, being older and perhaps wiser, I think the excitement overdone. We may gladly grant that recent times have taught us much and that the future will undoubtedly teach us more. And certainly we may boast, with justifiable pride, that we are in a position to correct earlier commentators in any number of ways, above all regarding Jesus' first-century Jewish world. This has indeed been a remarkably fruitful era in the study of Christian origins. In many ways, we do indeed know more than ever before.

At the same time, it seems unlikely that anything radically new regarding Jesus will be suggested in the future, or at least anything that is new and plausible. Moreover, and as already indicated, the prospect of a consensus on the key issues regarding Jesus is probably a utopian dream, as credible as the meek inheriting the earth. Furthermore, unrealistic aspirations and inadequate means beset much of the current activity. In the closing pages of Chapter One I questioned the wisdom of drawing clear-cut distinctions between authentic and inauthentic materials, although this has been and remains the goal of so much scholarship. Isolating Jesus from his interpreters may be as impractical as separating object and perceiver in quantum mechanics. Here in this chapter I should like to argue that, even if one dismisses my doubts and still wishes to unfasten Jesus from his interpreters, the usual procedures for doing this are defective.

The Wrong Tools for the Wrong Job

Scholars have, since the 1960s, often discussed the so-called criteria of authenticity, the sieves by which we supposedly enable ourselves to pan for original nuggets from Jesus. The names of the chief criteria are now well known: multiple attestation, dissimilarity, embarrassment, coherence. While they all at first glance appeal to common sense, further scrutiny reveals that they are fatally flawed. Dissimilarity, which allows us to hold as authentic items that are dissimilar to characteristic emphases of Judaism and of the church, presupposes that we know far more about the church and Judaism than we do. Multiple attestation overlooks the obvious problem that the more something is attested, the more the early church must have liked it, so the more suspicious we may well be about it.

I do not, however, wish to review here the defects of the traditional criteria. Those failings have become increasingly apparent over the last two decades, and much of the discussion is becoming tedious because repetitious: we have entered an echo chamber. I also wish to say little about recent suggestions for revising our criteria — a trick I was still trying to perform ten years ago — or about replacing them with new and improved criteria. My question is not Which criteria are good and which bad? or How should we employ the good ones? but rather Should we be using criteria at all?

My answer is No. In taking this position, I am setting myself against the dominant academic tradition, which has sought to find which bits of our texts represent Jesus' own views. Some may well wonder whether we are good for anything if we cannot sandblast the ecclesiastical soot from the tradition and restore the original. Others, perhaps suffering from a bit of physics envy, may insist that rigorously applying criteria is our only hope for keeping our discipline scientific and avoiding wholesale subjectivity. I am of a different mind.

After years of being in the quest business, I have reluctantly concluded that most of the Gospel materials are not subject to historical proof or disproof, or even to accurate estimates of their probability. That Jesus said something is no cause for supposing that we can demonstrate that he said it, and that Jesus did not say something is no cause for supposing that we can show that he did not say it. Similarly, if Jesus did something, that does not mean we can ascertain with any probability that he did it, and if he did not do something, that does not mean we can ascertain with any probability that he did not do it. There is a gaping chasm between what happened and what we can discover or deem likely to have happened. Put otherwise, the set of materials whose origin we can reasonably assign to Jesus or the church is scarcely identical with the set of materials the tradition credits to Jesus. The former is instead a subset of the latter, and a small one at that.

Did Jesus utter the golden rule? I do not see how anyone will ever show that he did, nor how anyone will ever show that he did not. I certainly have never run across persuasive arguments for one conclusion or the other. Sadly, this example is for me representative.

Casting aside, for the sake of argument, the warnings of Chapter One, let us assume that we can somehow drop every saying attributed to Jesus into one of three categories: (1) the authentic words, (2) the inauthentic words, and (3) the words whose origin we cannot determine — the possibly authentic or (if one prefers) the possibly inauthentic. A few sayings appear to commend themselves as good candidates for category (1), that is, as likely coming from Jesus, either because Paul and the Gospels both attest to them — one thinks of the prohibition of divorce (1 Cor. 7:10-11) — or because church invention is wildly implausible: surely Christians did not invent the accusation that Jesus was a glutton and drunkard. Other items betray themselves as likely secondary because they are redactional apologetic — Jesus persuading a reluctant John to baptize him (Matt. 3:15) comes to mind — or because they imply a date long after Jesus' death, an example being the line in Matthew's parable of the wedding banquet that adverts to the destruction of Jerusalem in AD 70: "the king . . . sent his troops, destroyed those murderers, and burned their city" (22:7).

Such easy judgments are, however, the exception. Category (3) outnumbers categories (1) and (2) put together. Who has mounted or can mount a compelling case for the authorship of the tale of the rich man and Lazarus in Luke 16:19-31, or of the parable of the wicked tenants in Mark 12:1-12, or of the picture of the sheep and goats at the last judgment in Matt. 25:31-46? Regarding these and so many other traditions, scholars cannot persuade others of differing views because their arguments are far from convincing. Our desire to know something does not mean that we can know it.

Scholars often work with the assumption that they should be able to inform us whether Jesus said X or whether he did not do Y. But we have too much self-esteem, too much confidence in our own abilities. We do not own the sleuthing talents of Sherlock Holmes. We are in truth more like Dr. Watson, whose plausible guesses were so often wrong. In my case, at least, experience has tamed ambition.

Repeatedly I have looked at a complex in the Jesus tradition and weighed the arguments on both sides — and there are almost always arguments pro and con, usually good arguments pro and con — and have been unable to acquire deep conviction one way or the other. Even when I have thought the scale tipped to this side rather than that, I have been aware that others perceive the matter differently. Again and again I have recalled a phrase used in the philosophy of science — "the underdetermination of theory by data."

We can ask questions that we cannot answer, or which can be plausibly answered in more than one way. Who wrote Hebrews? Many have argued for this or that candidate — Barnabas, Apollos, Priscilla. But of course no compelling argument is forthcoming, for the evidence does not suffice to establish anything beyond speculation. It is more often than not the same with the sayings in the Jesus tradition. Did Jesus admonish his hearers with, "Do not throw your pearls before swine" (Matt. 7:6)? Maybe, maybe not. Did he utter the woe against the rich in Luke 6:24? Who truly knows? We cannot establish any real probability on these matters, much less concoct some sort of rigorous demonstration. Historical analysis is not all-seeing or all-powerful; it can establish only so much.

It seems almost trite to say so, but it needs to be said: the fragmentary and imperfect nature of the evidence as well as the limitations of our historical-critical abilities should move us to confess, if we are conscientious, how hard it is to recover the past. Too often we cannot erase our ignorance. To use the current jargon, we frequently meet equifinity, the circumstance that a single state of affairs, in our case a text, can be plausibly accounted for by telling several very different stories. Origen knew the truth long ago when he confessed how exceedingly difficult it can be to show that a recorded event took place, even if it did take place.[1]

Many have remarked, with some chagrin, on the sundry conclusions of academics writing books and articles on the historical Jesus. The lack of unanimity bothers me less than it may others, for historical and religious studies belong not to the sciences but to the humanities, and waiting for a consensus on any noteworthy subject within the latter is like waiting for Godot. The main point here, however, is that the traditional criteria, which were devised as checks and balances for our subjectivity, have not delivered. The scope of diversity proves that we are still as embedded as ever in that subjectivity. All our methodological erudition, our repeated attempts to refine and heed criteria, have failed to impose order on our discipline: the Jesus of one book often does not look much like the Jesus of another book, even when those books employ more or less the same method. Surely we are no closer to any uniformity of results today than we would have been had we never heard of dissimilarity, multiple attestation, coherence, and embarrassment.

Doing history, which is an art requiring imagination and conjecture,

---

1. Origen, *Contra Celsum* 1.41.

cannot be identified with the mechanical observance of directives. The rules of chemistry mean that, if you follow the instructions, you will get the same result as everybody else. The criteria of authenticity are more like the rules of language: you can use them to say just about anything.

It is striking that, while the Jesus Seminar has used criteria of authenticity to dissociate John's Gospel from the historical Jesus, Craig Blomberg, a conservative New Testament scholar, can defend the historicity of John's Gospel by invoking closely-related criteria.[2] The current tools allow for radically different calculations of the ratio of memory to forgetfulness, of history to legend.

Because our criteria are not strong enough to resist our wills, we almost inevitably make them do what we want them to do: we, with our expectations and preconceptions, bend them more than they bend us. Certainly we are always working with some larger picture of Jesus and some theory about Christian origins, and so we are usually inclined to a certain result. How could it be otherwise? It is not that we are consciously being dishonest, just that the generalization of T. C. Chamberlin concerning scientists holds too for New Testament scholars. Once we adopt a theory,

> there is an unconscious selection and magnifying of the phenomena that fall into harmony with the theory and support it, and an unconscious neglect of those that fail of coincidence. The mind lingers with pleasure upon the facts that fall happily into the embrace of the theory, and feels a natural coldness toward those that seem refractory.... There springs up, also, an unconscious pressing of the theory to make it fit the facts and the facts to make them fit the theory. ... The search for facts, the observation of phenomena and their interpretation, are all dominated by affection for the favored theory until it appears to ... its advocate to have been overwhelmingly established. The theory then rapidly rises to the ruling position, and investigation, observation, and interpretation are controlled and directed by it.[3]

2. Craig L. Blomberg, *The Historical Reliability of John's Gospel: Issues and Commentary* (Downers Grove, IL: InterVarsity, 2001).

3. T. C. Chamberlin, "The Method of Multiple Working Hypotheses," *Science* 148 (1965): 755.

When you make a trap, you know exactly what you are looking for, and I suspect that it is usually the same with us when we comb through the Jesus tradition with criteria in hand. We wield our criteria to get what we want.

Although all this may sound cynical, it is my bet that, if my colleagues search their souls, they will recognize themselves in my words. When the criteria become the instruments through which we scrutinize the tradition, we are rarely surprised or nonplussed by the results. We are instead rooting for some particular outcome, and we are seldom disappointed.

My guess is that most New Testament scholars form a fairly clear picture of Jesus near the start of their careers, a picture that, while it may undergo some modification in subsequent years, rarely loses its basic features. Once a paradigm about Jesus is in place, a cognitive bias will also be in place. We all see what we expect to see and what we want to see; and if we hold a belief, we will notice confirming evidence. Disconfirming evidence will, to the contrary, make us uncomfortable, and so we will be more likely to miss, neglect, or critically evaluate it. This is the psychological reality within which we deploy our criteria.

Honesty moves me to indict myself here. Rightly or wrongly, for good reason or bad, I decided, sometime in college, that Jesus is best characterized as an apocalyptic prophet. I found Schweitzer more credible than C. H. Dodd, Jeremias more persuasive than Crossan. Despite, moreover, all that I have learned since, I remain of the same mind. My Jesus is the same yesterday, today, and probably forever. In my doctoral dissertation, he is an apocalyptic prophet. In my commentary on Matthew, he is an apocalyptic prophet. In my first book on Jesus, *Jesus of Nazareth: Millenarian Prophet,* he is an apocalyptic prophet. And no one will be surprised to learn that, in a forthcoming book, he remains an apocalyptic prophet.

Yet while, throughout the body of my work, Jesus fails to vary much, my method for finding him has changed. My dissertation and my commentary on Matthew (especially the first two volumes) employ, with little suspicion, the traditional criteria of authenticity (which the Jesus Seminar used to come to very different conclusions). In contrast, *Jesus of Nazareth* explicitly proposes a different approach, one that revises and relativizes those criteria. In more recent contributions, I have altogether set aside running individual items through criteria. And yet the Jesus of my first book is the Jesus of my last book. How can this be? Results, one might suppose, are determined by method. In my case, however, different methods, with and without criteria of authenticity, have produced the same result.

Whether or not one regards my experience as anomalous or as typical, surely none of us ever starts from scratch with criteria of authenticity or begins by establishing ground rules we then obey. A historian's Jesus is never just the consequence of reading sources through a screen of criteria. Rather, we conduct our intellectual rituals, that is, invent and/or apply our criteria, only after we have adopted some firm ideas about Jesus. Our criteria are less routes to our destination than ways of persuading others to end up where we have. E. P. Sanders once noted, with reference to the Apostle Paul, the difficulty of "distinguishing between the reasons for which he held a view and the arguments he adduces in favor of it."[4] Are we any different?

Maybe, to change the comparison, we are a bit like Christian apologists who muster arguments for believing in a supreme being. Such individuals typically believe in God because they were taught to believe, either by their parents or by a religious community. Only later, when encountering people without faith, do they investigate the history of philosophy and decide, let us say, that some version of the teleological or cosmological argument works. The attempted justification of their belief cannot be equated with the biographical reasons for it. Maybe New Testament scholars are not so different when it comes to Jesus.

Some versions of our standard criteria, I concede, usefully explicate what many of us have been doing instinctively all along. They nonetheless cannot transform us into scientists or overcome our subjectivity; and as they can and have justified very different reconstructions, one wants to know if there is not some better way of assuring ourselves of what the historical Jesus was about. Can we do nothing except trawl through the tradition with the criteria of authenticity?

4. E. P. Sanders, *Paul, the Law, and the Jewish People* (Philadelphia: Fortress, 1983), p. 4.

The General and the Particular

My own suggestion is that we approach the issue by reflecting on human memory, which constantly sins against us. It takes only a little honest introspection to reveal what modern researchers have now confirmed repeatedly, that we mix memories with imagination, that we assimilate one remembered event to another, that we find most of our memories dimming as time advances, that we distort recall to serve our own interests, that we impose narrative conventions on past events in order to make them intelligible, that we forget what we want or need to forget, that we see the past through the present, projecting current circumstances and beliefs backward in time, that we sometimes rewrite our own accurate memories out of deference to others with inferior memories, and that we can even "remember" events that never happened.

These facts should unsettle those of us who want to know about Jesus. We need not be bottomless skeptics to see that our sources have not been miraculously immune to all the usual failures and biases of memory. All one has to do is peruse a synopsis, which will reveal variations in order, contradictions in description, and discrepancies in wording. The New Testament preserves, for instance, four different accounts of what Jesus said and did at the Last Supper, and the substantial differences among them are notorious. Again, we have two reports of the Lord's Prayer, and they are scarcely identical. Christian memory was inexact even when it came to its foundational rites and prayers.

All this does not, however, render the quest hopeless. Even when human memory fails to retain the particulars, it can still get general impressions right. You may forget exactly what someone said to you and nevertheless remember the gist of it. Similarly, eyewitnesses may disagree on the details of a car wreck, but they will all agree that there was one. Memory may drop details or replace them with fictional details, but remembered feelings and generalities are less subject to deterioration and distortion. We can retain the meaning or impression of an event or conversation without retaining minutiae. As one researcher has put it,

> with passing of time, the particulars fade and opportunities multiply for interference — generated by later, similar experiences — to blur our recollections. We thus rely ever more on our memories for the gist of what happened, or what usually happens, and at-

tempt to reconstruct the details by inference and even sheer guesswork. Transience involves a gradual switch from reproductive and specific recollections to reconstructive and more general descriptions.[5]

Given that we typically remember the outlines of an event or the general purport of a conversation rather than the particulars and that we extract patterns and meaning from our memories, it makes little sense to open the quest for Jesus by evaluating individual items with our criteria, in the hope that some bits preserve pristine memory. We should rather be looking for repeating patterns and contemplating the big picture. We should trust first, if we are to trust at all, what is most likely to be trustworthy.

Although we may, after reading Thucydides, be confident that there was a Peloponnesian War, we may well wonder about many of the details of his account. The larger the generalization and the more data upon which it is based, the greater our confidence; the more specific the detail and the fewer the data supporting it, the more room we have for doubt.

With regard to the sources for Jesus, the traditional criteria of authenticity privilege the parts over the whole. It seems more prudent to privilege generalizations drawn from the whole than to concentrate upon one individual item after another. As a demonstration of how this works in practice, consider the following traditions:

- Jesus prohibited divorce: 1 Cor. 7:10; Mark 10:2-9; Luke 16:18.
- Jesus sent forth missionaries without staff, food, or money: Matt. 10:9-10; Mark 6:8-9; Luke 10:4.
- Jesus instructed missionaries to get their living by the gospel: 1 Cor. 9:14; Matt. 10:10; Luke 10:7.
- Jesus commanded loving and doing good to enemies: Matt. 5:38-48; Luke 6:27-36.
- Jesus forbade judging others: Matt. 7:1-2; Luke 6:37-38.
- Jesus asked a prospective follower not to bury his father: Matt. 8:21-22; Luke 9:59-60.

5. Daniel L. Schacter, *The Seven Sins of Memory: How the Mind Forgets and Remembers* (Boston/New York: Houghton Mifflin, 2001), pp. 15-16.

- Jesus spoke of hating one's father and mother: Matt. 10:37; Luke 14:26; *Gospel of Thomas* 55, 101.
- Jesus enjoined disciples to take up a cross: Matt. 10:38; Mark 8:34; Luke 14:27.
- Jesus enjoined unlimited forgiveness: Matt. 18:21-22; Luke 17:3-4.
- Jesus exhorted hearers to lose their lives in order to save them: Matt. 10:39; Mark 8:35; Luke 17:33.
- Jesus called people away from their livelihoods: Mark 1:16-20; 2:14.
- Jesus figuratively demanded violent removal of hand, foot, and eye: Mark 9:42-48.
- Jesus asked a wealthy man to relinquish his money: Mark 10:17-27.
- Jesus forbade taking oaths: Matt. 5:33-37.
- Jesus commanded money to be lent without interest: Matt. 5:42; *Gospel of Thomas* 95.
- Jesus called some to a life without marriage: Matt. 19:11-12.
- Jesus asked a prospective follower not to say farewell to his parents: Luke 9:61-62.
- Jesus asked his disciples to renounce all of their possessions: Luke 14:33.

I infer from this collection of materials that Jesus made uncommonly difficult demands on at least some people. Whatever he may have taught about compassion, and whether or not his motivation owed something to eschatological expectation, he insisted on self-sacrifice, to the point of demanding that some individuals follow him immediately and unconditionally.

This historical verdict holds whatever tradition histories one draws up for the various units. What matters is not whether we can establish the authenticity of any of the relevant traditions or what the criteria of authenticity may say about them, but rather the pattern that they, in concert, create. It is like running into students who enjoy telling tales about their absent-minded professor. A number of those tales may be too tall to earn our belief; but if there are several of them, they are good evidence that the professor is indeed absent-minded.

Working through the tradition in the way I suggest leads to a large number of conclusions. Jesus must have been an exorcist who interpreted his ministry in terms of Satan's downfall. He must have thought highly of John the Baptist. He must have repeatedly spoken of God as Father. He must have composed parables. He must have come into conflict with religious authorities.

All of this may seem obvious, but the procedure is not trite, for it also issues in some controversial verdicts. As I have argued elsewhere, for example, the quantity of conventional eschatological material in our primary sources almost necessitates that Jesus was an eschatological prophet.[6] The reconstruction of Robert Funk and the Jesus Seminar is for this reason alone problematic.

Even more controversial is what my approach leads me to infer about Jesus' self-conception. Consider these Synoptic materials:

- Jesus said that the Son of man will return on the clouds of heaven and send angels to gather the elect from throughout the world: Mark 13:26-27; cf. 14:62; Matt. 10:23 (allusions to Daniel 7's depiction of the last judgment are clear).
- The sons of Zebedee asked to sit at the right and left hand of Jesus and so presupposed his eschatological enthronement: Mark 10:35-40; cf. 14:62.
- Jesus selected a group of twelve disciples, whose number must represent the tribes of Israel (cf. Matt. 19:28); and as he was not among their number but instead their leader, his leadership of renewed Israel is implied: Mark 3:13-19.
- Peter thought that Jesus must be "the Messiah": Mark 8:29; cf. 14:61-62.
- Jesus declared that the fate of at least some individuals at the final assize will depend on whether they have acknowledged or denied him: Mark 8:38; Matt. 10:32-33; Luke 12:8-9.
- When Jesus went up to Jerusalem, crowds hailed him with the words, "Hosanna! Blessed is the one who comes in the name of the Lord! Blessed is the coming kingdom of our ancestor David": Mark 11:9-10.
- Jesus prophesied that he would destroy and rebuild the temple: Mark 14:58.
- When the chief priest asked Jesus whether he was "the Messiah," he replied by applying Dan. 7:13 and Ps. 110:1 to himself: Mark 14:61-62.

---

6. Dale C. Allison, Jr., *Constructing Jesus: Memory and Imagination* (Grand Rapids, MI: Baker Academic, 2009). See also below, pp. 90-96.

- The Roman governor Pilate asked Jesus whether he took himself to be "the king of the Jews," and Jesus did not say "No": Mark 15:2.
- Jesus called himself "Lord" and warned that not to do what he commanded will bring personal destruction: Matt. 7:21-27; Luke 6:46-49.
- Jesus, in response to a query from John the Baptist, equated himself with the latter's "coming one": Matt. 11:2-4 = Luke 7:18-23 (the answer draws on prophetic texts in Isaiah and makes an implicit claim to fulfill them).
- Jesus warned cities rejecting him — not John the Baptist or someone else — that they will suffer for it at the eschatological judgment: Matt. 10:15; 11:21-24; Luke 10:12-15.
- Jesus avowed that people who "receive" his disciples really "receive" him, and that to "receive" him is to receive the one who sent him, God: Matt. 10:40; Luke 10:16.
- Jesus interpreted his success in casting out demons "by the finger of God" — an allusion to Exod. 8:19 that makes him Mosaic — to mean that God's kingdom had arrived; he thereby made himself out to be the chief means or manifestation of its arrival: Matt. 12:28; Luke 11:20.
- Jesus assured his followers that they will "judge" — which means either "rule" or "pass judgment on" — restored Israel, and he cannot have thought of his role as any less: Matt. 19:28; Luke 22:28-30.
- Jesus read from the beginning of Isaiah 61 and proclaimed that its prophecies were fulfilled in his ministry; he thus claimed to be the anointed prophet of Isaiah's eschatological vision: Luke 4:16-19.

As with the argument about Jesus making extraordinary demands, so here too: I do not contend (or deny) that Jesus formulated any of the sayings just cited, or that any event or circumstance referred to must be deemed historical. I am rather displaying a pattern. Jesus' starring role in the eschatological drama is all over the tradition, in words attributed to him and in words assigned to others, in stories as well as in sayings. Mark firmly attests to it. So also does the material common to Matthew and Luke but not in Mark. So too traditions unique to Matthew and Luke. And it would be easy enough to add material from Paul, Acts, John, the *Gospel of Thomas,* and elsewhere. So my inference is that, whatever titles he may or may not have used, Jesus probably believed himself to be not just an eschatological prophet but the personal locus of the end-time scenario, the central figure of the last judgment, someone akin to

Melchizedek in 11QMelchizedek, or the Elect One in the Parables of *1 Enoch.*

My manner of argument will seem to many to be far too easy, indeed simplistic, and a turning back the clock to less critical days. My defense, however, is this. If the primary sources produce false general impressions, such as that Jesus was an apocalyptic prophet when he was not, or that Jesus was Israel's redeemer when he had no such thought, then the truth of things is almost certainly beyond our reach. If the chief witnesses are too bad, if they contain only intermittently authentic items, we cannot lay them aside and tell a better story. Given how memory works, how could we ever feel at ease with a Jesus who is much different from the individual on the surface of our texts? Wrong in general, wrong in the particulars. In order for us to find Jesus, our sources must often remember at least the sorts of things he did and the sorts of things that he said, including what he said about himself. If the repeating patterns do not catch Jesus, then how can he not forever escape us?

Although there is a canonical bias in all this, it is unavoidable. Because the Synoptics supply us with most of our first-century traditions, our reconstructed Jesus will inevitably be Synoptic-like, a sort of commentary on Matthew, Mark, and Luke. Nothing else, however, can carry conviction. If we insist instead on countering in significant ways the general impressions left by our early sources, the pictures we paint in their place will be like sidewalk drawings done in chalk: we may delight in making them, and others may enjoy looking at them, but they will not last very long.

Although this conclusion is, from one point of view, what one might consider conservative, from another it is not. I remain skeptical that we can very often show that any particular saying or story goes back to Jesus or does not go back to him. We need to quit pretending to do what we cannot do. The Gospels are parables. When we read them, we should think not that Jesus said this or did that but rather: Jesus did things like this, and he said things like that.

Miracles Here, There, and Everywhere

Jesus is, throughout the tradition, a miracle worker. Here is a list of relevant materials:

- The devil assumes that Jesus has miraculous powers: Matt. 4:1-11; Luke 4:1-13.
- Jesus heals a centurion's servant or son: Matt. 8:5-13; Luke 7:1-10.
- Jesus recites a list of his own miracles: Matt. 11:2-5; Luke 7:18-23.
- Jesus instructs followers to cure the sick: Matt. 10:8; Luke 10:9; *Gospel of Thomas* 14.
- Jesus rebukes cities for not responding favorably to his "wonders": Matt. 11:21; Luke 10:13.
- Jesus says that he casts out demons: Matt. 12:27-28; Luke 11:19-20.
- Jesus promises that faith can work miracles: Matt. 17:20; Luke 17:6; Mark 11:22-23.
- Jesus casts out demons from a man in the synagogue: Mark 1:21-28.
- Jesus heals Peter's mother-in-law: Mark 1:29-31.
- Jesus heals a leper: Mark 1:40-45.
- Jesus heals a paralytic: Mark 2:1-12.
- Jesus restores a withered hand: Mark 3:1-6.
- Jesus instructs his disciples to cast out demons: Mark 3:15.
- Jesus heals a blind and mute demoniac: Matt. 12:22-32.
- Jesus calms a storm: Mark 4:35-41.
- Jesus cures a demoniac: Mark 5:1-20.
- Jesus raises Jairus's daughter: Mark 5:21-24, 35-43.
- Jesus heals a bleeding woman: Mark 5:25-34.
- Jesus feeds five thousand: Mark 6:30-44; John 6:1-15.
- Jesus walks on water: Mark 6:45-51; John 6:16-21.
- Jesus casts out demons from a Canaanite woman's daughter: Mark 7:24-30.
- Jesus heals a deaf mute: Mark 7:31-37.
- Jesus feeds four thousand: Mark 8:1-10.
- Jesus restores sight to a blind man: Mark 8:22-26.
- Jesus is transfigured into light: Mark 9:2-8.
- Jesus casts out demons from a boy: Mark 9:14-29.
- Jesus cures a blind man: Mark 10:46-52.
- Jesus curses a fig tree which withers: Mark 11:12-14, 20-24.
- Jesus heals two blind men: Matt. 9:27-31.
- Jesus heals a deaf demoniac: Matt. 9:32-34.
- Jesus has Peter catch a fish with a coin in its mouth: Matt. 17:24-27.
- Jesus directs a miraculous haul of fish: Luke 5:1-11.
- Jesus raises a widow's son: Luke 7:11-17.

- Jesus heals a crippled woman: Luke 13:10-17.
- Jesus heals a man with dropsy: Luke 14:1-6.
- Jesus heals ten lepers: Luke 17:11-19.
- Jesus heals a severed ear: Luke 22:50-51.
- Jesus turns water into wine: John 2:1-12.
- Jesus knows a woman's history without being told: John 4:17-18.
- Jesus heals a lame man: John 5:1-18.
- Jesus heals a blind man: John 9:1-12.
- Jesus raises Lazarus: John 11.
- Jesus was "a doer of incredible wonderful deeds" (παραδόξων ἔργων): Josephus, *Antiquities* 18.63.
- Jesus "practiced sorcery": *b. Sanhedrin* 43a.

In addition to these many items, there are the Evangelists' summarizing reports, which repeatedly stress that Jesus healed people: Matt. 4:23-25; Mark 3:7-12; Luke 5:15; John 20:30, etc.

Preternatural wonders are on almost every page of the primary sources. Those who think like David Hume and doubt or do not believe that such wonders can occur might suppose that the miracle-ridden nature of our sources defeats my method, which posits that we can be confident of finding Jesus above all in the repeating patterns. If, one might argue, miracles do not happen, then Jesus did not do miracles, so here is an instance where a repeating pattern must be the product not of reliable memory but of early Christian fancy.

Miracles are of course a problem for any who want to find much memory in the Gospels. The quest itself got underway in the eighteenth century when the deists, turning their quarrels with the church into quarrels with the Bible, asked: How can we credit the Gospels when they are so full of incredible miracles? The deists did not much credit them.

Even if we are not disciples of Hume or adherents of a materialistic scientism, it remains hard for many of us moderns not to fret about the astounding stories attributed to Jesus. Do we not know that tradition always exaggerates and that a tendency to mythomania seems to be part of human nature? How can anyone with a good education wholeheartedly believe that Jesus walked on water, that he fed five thousand with a few food scraps, or that he restored the dead to the land of the living? Such incredible things seem opposed to ordinary human experience. Similar things do, however, often appear in archaic tales that everybody knows to be fictional — the apocryphal gospels, for instance — tales that once fed what appears to have been an insatiable craving for the marvelous. It is no mystery why Reimarus, Strauss, and Bultmann regarded the miracle stories of the Gospels as pious fictions. They were just being reasonable — and treating the Gospels the same way that the rest of us treat the fantastic fables of the Greek gods. One understands the modern habit of preferring, on principle, natural causes to miraculous causes.

Consider the transfiguration. How can we receive it as sober history? Jewish legend bestowed radiance upon Adam, Enoch, Noah, Abraham, and a host of others. Christian imagination similarly moved the artistic nimbi decorating the icons of the saints into their sacred biographies. There are, for example, stories about some of the desert fathers shining, and Roman Catholic tradition is full of shining saints, Francis of Assisi being perhaps the most famous.

As if that were not enough to engender doubt, the story of Jesus' transfiguration can be explained in part as a rewriting of the story of Moses on Sinai. Jesus, like Moses, is transfigured on a mountain (Exod. 34:29-30, 35; Mark 9:2-3). In both cases a cloud descends (Exod. 24:15-18; 34:5; Mark 9:7), and in both a divine voice issues from the cloud (Exod. 24:16; Mark 9:7). Those who see the radiance of Jesus become afraid, just as do those who behold Moses aglow (Exod. 34:30; Mark 9:6). The transfiguration of Jesus takes place "after six days" (Mark 9:2), and Moses climbs Sinai after six days of preparation (Exod. 24:16). Besides the seventy elders, Moses takes with him three confidential friends, Aaron, Nadab, and Abihu (Exod. 24:1, 9-11); Jesus climbs his mountain with Peter, James, and John (Mark 9:2). Finally, the voice that claims Jesus with "This is my beloved Son; listen to him," echoes the oracle in Deut. 18:15, 18, which foresees a prophet like Moses to whom the people are to "listen."

We need also to keep firmly before our minds that it was a habit of the early Christians to score theological points by inventing fantastic, picturesque stories. The following flight of imagination appears in *The Acts of Peter and Andrew*. I quote it in full, so that it might have its full effect:

> There was a certain rich man . . . named Onesiphorus. Having seen the miracles done through the apostles, he said: "If I believe in your God, will I be able to do a miracle as you do?" Andrew said to him, "If you give up all of your possessions and your wife and your children, as we have given them up, then you also will do

miracles." Hearing this, Onesiphorus became angry, and he took his towel and put it around Andrew's neck and struck him and said to him, "You are a sorcerer. How is it that you force me to abandon my wife and children and goods?"

Then Peter, turning and seeing him hitting Andrew, said to him, "Man, stop hitting Andrew." Onesiphorus said to him, "I see that you are more reasonable than he is. Are you also going to tell me to leave my wife and my children and my goods? What do you say?" Peter said to him, "This one word I say to you, 'It is easier for a camel to go through the eye of a needle than for a rich person to enter into the kingdom of heaven.'" When Onesiphorus heard these things, he was all the more filled with anger and wrath, and he took his towel off of Andrew's neck and put it around Peter's neck, and then he dragged him along, saying, "Truly you are a greater sorcerer than the other one, for a camel cannot go through the eye of a needle. But if you show me this wonder, I will believe in your God, and not I alone, but also the whole city. But if not, you will be greatly punished in the midst of the city."

Hearing these things, Peter was exceedingly grieved, and standing and stretching forth his hands to heaven he prayed, saying, "Master, Lord our God, hearken to me in this hour, for they will entrap us by your own words. For no prophet or patriarch has clarified the interpretation [of your saying] . . . that we might learn its explanation. And now they seek from us its interpretation. . . . Do not then, Master, overlook us. For you are the one hymned by the cherubim."

After he said this, the Savior appeared in the form of a child of twelve years old . . . and he said to them, "Take heart and do not tremble. . . . Let the needle and the camel be brought." After saying this, he went up into heaven. Now there was a certain merchant in the city who had believed in the Lord through the Apostle Philip. When (that merchant) heard these things, he ran and sought for a needle with a big eye, to do a favor for the apostles. When Peter learned this, he said, "My son, do not search for a big needle. For nothing is impossible with God. Instead bring us a very thin needle."

After the needle was brought, and all the multitude of the city stood around to see, Peter looked up and saw a camel coming.

And he ordered her to be brought. Then he fixed the needle in the ground and, crying out with a loud voice, said, "In the name of Jesus Christ, who was crucified under Pontius Pilate, I command you, O camel, that you go through the eye of the needle." Then the eye of the needle was opened like a gate, and the camel went through it. And all the multitude saw it. Again Peter said to the camel, "Go again through the needle." And the camel went a second time.

Seeing these things, Onesiphorus said to Peter, "Truly you are a great sorcerer. Yet I will not believe unless I send and bring a camel and a needle." And calling one of his servants, he said to him secretly, "Go and bring to me here a camel and a needle. Find also a sin-stained woman, and mount her on (the camel) and compel her to come here; and (bring also) a carcass of pigskin. For these men are sorcerers."

Peter, having learned the mystery through the Spirit, said to Onesiphorus, "O hard-hearted man, send and bring the camel and the woman and the needle with the carcass."

When they had brought them, Peter again took the needle and fixed it in the ground along with the carcass. And the woman was sitting on the camel. Then Peter said, "In the name of our Lord Jesus Christ the crucified, I order you, O camel, to go through this needle." Immediately the eye of the needle was opened and became like a gate, and the camel went through it. Peter again said to the camel, "Go through it again, that all may see the glory of our Lord Jesus Christ, in order that some may believe in him." Then the camel again went through the needle.

Seeing these things, Onesiphorus cried out with a great voice saying, "Truly great is the God of Peter and Andrew, and I from now on will believe in the name of our Lord Jesus Christ."

The author of this vivid and outlandish fantasy had to know, while he was making it all up, that he was making it all up. Further, his far-fetched tale so sacrifices all probability for the sake of delight in storytelling that later hearers or readers must have known this too. Certainly rabbinic literature, in which authoritative commentary regularly comes from Elijah or a heavenly voice, has its share of obviously fictional anecdotes that were never intended to be sober history. Is it not, then, natural to suppose that some or even many of the miracle stories about Jesus were likewise composed to teach theological lessons, not record historical facts? Surely some of them, even if they go back to things that happened, are now draped with supernatural overlay such as the dove and voice at the baptism. And surely other stories are the products of theological fancy in which the history is of homeopathic proportions. Excellent candidates for the last category include Matthew's infancy narrative, Peter walking on the water (Matt. 14:28-33), and the many corpses stirring to life at Jesus' crucifixion (Matt. 27:51-53).

Is not the sensible verdict that the transfiguration is likewise not a report but a myth, whose meaning can have nothing to do with what really happened? The retort of the traditionalist — Jesus did extraordinary things because he was the supernatural figure the church has made him out to be, and the transfiguration just may be one such extraordinary thing — seems anemic in the face of the evidence.

And yet, having said all this, the judgment that the transfiguration is nothing but mythology may turn out to be premature. For the inference implicitly assumes that people are never transfigured into light, or at least that there are no credible accounts of such, whereas, if one patiently investigates without prejudice, one discovers a surprisingly large body of firsthand testimony reporting just this.

One witness is Gregory of Nyssa, the famous fourth-century Cappadocian father. In his eulogy of his brother Basil he wrote this: "At night, while he was at prayer in the house, there came a light, illuminating [Basil]; a certain immaterial light by divine power lit up the house, and it was without a material source."[7] Some might feel free to dismiss these words as ancient credulity, or maybe as a rhetorical flight of fancy. I hesitate, however. Not only was Gregory an extraordinarily intelligent man, but I have, over the years, formed an opinion of his character, and it is hard for me to discount his apparently earnest witness. It is easier for me to believe that he saw a light he could not explain, whatever its origin may have been.

Closer to our own time, we have a report concerning Seraphim of Sarov, the Russian Orthodox saint (1759-1833). As a hieromonk of pious reputation, he was regularly sought out by pilgrims at his cabin in the wilderness. One such was a man named Nicholas Motovilov, whose

---

7. Gregory of Nyssa, *Encomium of Saint Gregory* 10.1.

notes about Seraphim, recording their private encounters, were discovered in 1903. These notes contain the following:

> Then I looked at the Staretz and was panic-stricken. Picture, in the sun's orb, in the most dazzling brightness of its noon-day shining, the face of a man who is talking to you. You see his lips moving, the expression in his eyes, you hear his voice, you feel his arms round your shoulders, and yet you see neither his arms, nor his body, nor his face, you lose all sense of yourself, you can see only the blinding light which spreads everywhere, lighting up the layer of snow covering the glade, and igniting the flakes that are falling on us both like white powder.[8]

Perhaps the most interesting episode I have run across concerns Sri Sathya Sai Baba, the contemporary Hindu holy man. Several people have reported to western interviewers that in the late 1940s they saw him glowing at the top of a mountain. Here is one eyewitness's testimony, taken from her diary, written soon after the event it relates:

> All devotees had gathered at the bottom of the hill and were watching him. Already it was sunset. Sri Baba could be seen by all from there. Behind his head bright red rays, which resemble the rays of sunset, were shining. After some time, they disappeared and were replaced by a bright powerful light that was emanating . . . blinding sunrays and that was glistening like a diamond on the head of a snake. Looking at it and unable to tolerate the brightness, two people collapsed to the ground. All the people were staring with wide open eyes, overwhelmed with joy. Immediately the light disappeared and there was pitch darkness. . . . All our hearts were filled with joy. He went to the people who had collapsed and applied vibuti, which he had materialized in his hand, to their foreheads. They regained consciousness and offered salutations to him.[9]

This story, however one wishes to account for it, is indisputably firsthand.

8. Valentine Zander, *St. Seraphim of Sarov* (Crestwood, NY: St. Vladimir's Seminary Press, 1975), p. 91.

9. Erlendur Haraldsson, *Modern Miracles: An Investigative Report on Psychic Phenomena Associated with Sai Baba* (New York: Fawcett Columbine, 1987), p. 255.

The foregoing testimonies intrigue me all the more because I personally know a man who claims to have seen a human being transfigured into light. This is not for me a folktale, that is, it does not concern the proverbial friend-of-a-friend but comes to my ears from someone I know and have no reason to disbelieve (and who has refreshed my memory by kindly sharing with me his relevant journal entry).

In 1992 my friend John decided to seek initiation as a Sufi. The process involved having an audience with a Sufi master who was then making a tour of the States. The two men met in a small room for a short period of time. They sat face-to-face in lotus position. No words passed between them. But the occasion was memorable, for John relates that, after a bit, the master began to emit a light, which became brighter and brighter, until it lit up the whole room, after which the luminescence gradually faded away, and the encounter was over.

I honestly do not know how we should explain the stories I have just recounted. A religious individual of ecumenical sympathies might wish them all to be genuinely preternatural experiences. A parapsychologist might find here an ill-understood phenomenon inviting further investigation. A skeptic might assail the stories by guessing that my friend John hallucinated, that Sai Baba is an accomplished magician (there is indeed good evidence for this opinion), that Motovilov planned on publishing his memoirs and so felt a need to embellish them, and that Gregory of Nyssa's funeral rhetoric carried his memory past the facts.

None of which, however, is to my point, which concerns not explaining what really happened but only the fact that people have sincerely reported seeing others transfigured. The stories are in truth numerous. If one looks into Roman Catholic proceedings on canonization, one discovers any number of firsthand reports of shining saints, many of them from obviously earnest people.[10] Similarly sincere statements come from twentieth-century monks on Mount Athos.[11]

---

10. Herbert Thurston, *The Physical Phenomenon of Mysticism* (London: Burns Oates, 1952), pp. 162-70.

11. Alexander Golitzin, *The Living Witness of the Holy Mountain: Contemporary Voices from Mount Athos* (South Canaan, CT: St. Tikon's Seminary Press, 1996), pp. 34-54, 153-57, 194-215. Note also Carlos S. Alvarado, "Observations of Luminous Phenomena around the Human Body: A Review," *Journal of the Society for Psychical Research* 54 (1987): 38-60, and the collection of testimonies in Patricia Treece, *The Sanctified Body* (New York: Doubleday, 1989), pp. 64-85.

Returning to the transfiguration, what are we to think? On the one hand, legend delights in surrounding religious worthies with supernatural light, which should make us skeptical, and our skepticism should be augmented by the obvious literary dependence of the Gospel accounts on the traditions about the shining face of Moses. On the other hand, people do have visions, and sometimes they are (whatever the explanation) honestly convinced that they have seen someone wrapped by a supernatural aura. If, moreover, somebody recalled seeing such around Jesus, this might well have issued in a story like that in the Synoptics, with its typological relationship to Sinai. Early Jewish Christians lived and moved and had their being in the Scriptures, and it was their wont to write up events and stories so that they echo biblical narratives. That Eusebius, when he recounted the battle of the Milvian bridge, construed the event as a new exodus and turned Constantine into a new Moses (*Ecclesiastical History* 9.9) is not evidence that there was no battle of the Milvian bridge.

Our problem is that historians of the Gospels face two reasonable alternatives, and it is not clear how we are to decide which is better. I once thought that Peter's remark, "Rabbi, it is good for us to be here; let us make three dwellings, one for you, one for Moses, and one for Elijah" (Mark 9:5), argues for some historical basis, so intractable is it. But, as I now recognize in retrospect, this can hardly carry the day. One assumes that the disciple's unlikely suggestion, whose purport no one to my satisfaction has ever made out, meant something to someone at some point, otherwise the tradition would never have included it; and what justice is there in my supposing that only the historical Peter, as opposed to some later composer or tradent, could have strung together words whose sense now escapes us? So my argument for the transfiguration going back to an authentic visionary experience fails to persuade.

Do any observations favor the opposite conclusion, that the transfiguration is sheer fiction? One might insist that, even if odd things happen now and then, and even if people are sometimes perceived as radiant, the transfiguration is not an isolated miracle. The Gospels pour forth a cascade of miracles, each following another in rapid succession. Is this not a sure sign of myth as opposed to memory?

This is not the clincher one might initially imagine, because some saintly or charismatic individuals can become associated with multiple miracle stories, many told by firsthand witnesses. Thousands in present-day India believe that they have seen Sai Baba perform an impressive variety of miracles. In Italy, many yet living relate the wonders that allegedly accompanied Padre Pio, the Capuchin monk (1887-1968). Hundreds in the United States, during the 1950s, thought they had received divine healing by the hands of Kathryn Kuhlman or Oral Roberts, as did thousands who watched their services on television. And so it goes.

How should we explain all this? Gregory of Nyssa observed that most people judge what is credible by their own experience, which is fair enough.[12] One can look critically at the Jesus tradition and hold that what people then perceived as wonders we can explain in more mundane terms. Maybe some possessed individuals had psychosomatic disorders and responded to Jesus' renown as a successful exorcist. Or maybe some who encountered him had hysterical blindness, which disappeared through their faith in him. The power of suggestion is remarkable, as the study of placebos and nocebos has established. Furthermore, although this strategy is no longer the fashion within the guild, one might explain away some of the miracles as misperception. The Florida State University oceanographer who recently informed us that Jesus may have walked not on water but on a piece of floating ice was no more credible than those nineteenth-century critics, skewered by Strauss, who surmised that Jesus had not raised anyone from the dead but only lucked out: some comatose individuals woke up after he prayed over them. Nonetheless, amazing tales do often grow out of mundane misperceptions, as when people turn a bear into Bigfoot or look at an unusually bright star and mistake it for a UFO.

My point is that testimony is one thing, explanation another, and that the miracles associated with Jesus need not be late or secondary inventions. Many of them might derive from early times and (although we could never show this to be true) even come from firsthand witnesses. Paul claimed to have entered "the third heaven" (2 Cor. 12:1-5) and to have performed "signs and wonders and mighty works" (12:12). Josephus testified in writing: "I have seen a certain Eleazar, a countryman of mine, in the presence of Vespasian, his sons, tribunes and a number of other soldiers, free men possessed by demons" (*Antiquities* 8.46). Sulpicius Severus was a personal friend of Bishop Martin of Tours, about whom he composed a famous life which is filled with remarkable miracle stories. Au-

12. Gregory of Nyssa, *Life of Macrina* 39.

gustine, in *City of God* 22.8, narrates a slew of wonders performed during his lifetime, some of which he had personally witnessed, others of which he had learned about from eyewitnesses. Theodoret's *History of the Monks of Syria* is filled with miracle-working monks known to the author.

So a miracle story, just because it is a miracle story, is not necessarily late and unhistorical; and we have no reason, whatever our philosophical or religious disposition, to deny that people could have perceived or remembered Jesus doing miraculous things, or even a large number of miraculous things. Whether or not one believes that divinely-wrought miracles or paranormal events ever transpire, many have believed that they do, and many have thought themselves witnesses of events resembling those in the Synoptics, including the so-called nature miracles.

Having come to this conclusion, we have made only modest progress, for if any particular miracle story need not be the product of secondary or legendary development, that supplies no reason to embrace its historicity. More often than not, at least in my judgment, we are unable to determine the origin of a wonder. Is the account of Jesus feeding 5,000 a theological tale without historical occasion? Or does it, like the story of Jesus' baptism, overlay memories of a historical event — a large crowd flocked to Jesus in the desert — with a dramatic, supernatural prodigy — the inexplicable multiplication? Or is some less mundane explanation the truth? I see no way to decide between these options.

What we can confidently infer about the miracles of Jesus on the basis of modern historical criticism is that he was reputed to be and thought himself to be a successful exorcist, healer, and wonder-worker and that some who knew him believed that they had witnessed truly extraordinary events. It is also reasonable to surmise that the Synoptic stories give us a fair idea of how he went about casting out demons and healing the sick. But we cannot venture much further.

If we often cannot decide which miracle stories go back to historical events and which are free creations, we have arrived at the same place we did with the sayings tradition. Earlier I contended that, although we can make a number of valuable generalizations about Jesus from the larger patterns of the sayings taken as a whole, showing that Jesus uttered or did not utter a particular logion is very often beyond our ability. As with most of the sayings, so it is with most of the stories, including the miracle stories: their origin is not subject to our demonstration.

One final point about miracles. The argument from analogy has usually been employed to argue that the miracle stories in the Gospels are not memories but inventions. Being like so many obviously fictional tales, they likewise must be unhistorical. I have swapped this argument for another, urging instead that the numerous accounts of purported wonders from sincere eyewitnesses should moderate our skepticism and keep us open-minded.

Either argument from analogy, however, might leave a Christian feeling alienated. Are not the miracles intended to underline the unique status of Jesus? After all, the voice at the transfiguration does not say "You've seen this before," but instead claims: "This is my Son, the Beloved; listen to him" (Mark 9:7). How can the miracle stories inform us about Jesus' distinctive identity if, taking a comparative point of view, we limit ourselves to what the parallels allow as generally plausible? Is this not to reduce Jesus to what we know about others? And does not an exclusively historical analysis miss the literary and theological meaning of Jesus' miracles? Almost all of them are motivated by compassion, which characterizes the merciful God present and active in him. The Gospels also present Jesus' wonders as the fulfillment of prophecy. The inventory of miracles in Matt. 11:2-5 and Luke 7:18-23 is, for instance, designed to call to mind oracles from Isaiah and so imply that the eschatological age, when illness will vanish and all wrongs will be made right, has begun to arrive in Jesus' ministry (26:19; 29:18-19; 35:5-6; 42:18; 61:1-2). My discussion, however, has taken no notice of such charged facts.

My response is that I have had a single ambition in the previous pages, and it has been historical, not theological. My only concern has been to urge that the miracle tradition is not proof of a catastrophic memory failure in the early Jesus tradition. If, in so arguing, I have adhered to the principle of analogy, which serves historians so well but troubles many Christians, I can only plead guilty. I am a historian as well as a Christian, and I seek to be honest on both accounts.

Perhaps I am a bit like many churchgoing scientists who on Sunday confess belief in the "creator of heaven and earth" and yet, in their day-to-day work, follow, without undue interference from their religious faith, scientific and even reductionistic methods as they try to understand the natural world. Whether or not that is an appropriate analogy, I shall, in subsequent pages, try to think as a faithful Christian, just as I have tried, in this chapter, to think as a conscientious historian.

CHAPTER 4

Some Difficult Conclusions

"We instinctively recoil from seeing an object to which our emotions and affections are committed handled by the intellect as any other object is handled."

WILLIAM JAMES

"The human understanding when it has once adopted an opinion . . . draws all things else to support and agree with it. And though there be a greater number and weight of instances to be found on the other side, yet these it either neglects and despises, or else by some distinction sets aside and rejects, in order that by this great and pernicious predetermination the authority of its former conclusions may remain inviolate."

FRANCIS BACON

I have, in the previous pages, stressed the limitations of the quest of the historical Jesus. Reducing the theological Jesus to the historical Jesus is no more plausible than reducing the mental world to the physical world, even if a lot of smart people have tried to do both. When the historians are done, much is left undone, and the theologians are just getting started. I have also cautioned about easy appeals to any sort of consensus among scholars of the Bible. Truly assured results are few and the academic conflicts are many, and theologians must take great care when they seek to build upon the ground of modern criticism. Foundations can shift.

Perhaps some, persuaded that the church's Jesus and the historian's Jesus repel each other just like the identical poles of two magnets, may welcome my cautions. They may in fact find in them justification for altogether disregarding the quest, which they reckon pernicious. They cannot, however, abolish the quest: it will go on whether they like it or not and whether they are paying attention or not. Moreover, just because we cannot, peering across the darkness of two thousand years, do everything with the historical Jesus does not mean that we should do nothing with him. And just because some of the historians are wrong about much does not mean that all of them are wrong about everything.

The quest has not been all futile and inconclusive; indeed, reading the literature on the historical Jesus can change, as it has in my case, how one thinks about the Christian faith. In this chapter I should like to illustrate some ways in which this might happen.

Christology: Too Low and Too High

The New Testament depicts Jesus in two different ways. Many texts present him as a human being like the rest of us, a person of flesh and blood and of human psychology. He grows "in wisdom and in years and in divine and human favor" (Luke 2:52). He is tempted to do what he knows is wrong (Mark 1:12-13). He suffers, from which he learns (Heb. 5:8). He eats, thirsts, weeps, bleeds, and gets angry (Mark 3:5; 4:38; John 11:35; 19:28, 34). He asks questions (Mark 5:9, 30; 6:38; 8:23; 9:16, 21, 33). He admits that he does not know when the end will come (Mark 13:32). He prays to God, and in the face of death he must wrestle to annul his desire before the divine will (Mark 14:32-42). And, at the end, he dies, feeling that God has forsaken him (Mark 15:34).

All this seems straightforward enough: Jesus was, as Acts 2:22 plainly states, "a man" (ἀνήρ), a human being who struggled and doubted and knew some things, not others. There are, however, texts that depict Jesus as being unlike the rest of us, that push him out of the realm of humanity and into the sphere of the divine. Phil. 2:6-7 seemingly posits his preexistence. Mark 4:35-41 and 6:45-52 have him calm the waves and walk on the water, feats that the Old Testament assigns to God (Pss. 65:7; 77:19; 89:9; Job 9:8). Matt. 11:27 and Luke 10:22 quote Jesus as saying that the Son alone — not Abraham, not Moses, not David — knows the divine Father. John 8:58 has Jesus refer to himself with the loaded "I am" (ἐγώ εἰμί); 10:30 has him claim, "I and the Father are one"; and 14:9 puts on his lips the words, "The one who has seen me has seen the Father." Col. 1:15-19 teaches that Jesus is the visible image of the invisible God, in whom the fullness of God was pleased to dwell. Rev. 21:5-6 seats Jesus on God's throne (cf. 22:3, 13). John 20:28 has Thomas address Jesus as "My Lord and my God." And John 1:1 identifies Jesus as "the Word" (ὁ λόγος) which was "in the beginning" (ἐν ἀρχῇ) and which "was with God" (ἦν πρὸς τὸν θεόν) and which "was God" (θεὸς ἦν).

How might Christians account for and come to terms with the two different presentations of Jesus in their canonical sources? We usually characterize God and humanity by means of antithetical contrasts. One is creator, the other created. One is eternal, the other mortal. One is sinless, the other sinful. The truth of Num. 23:19 seems patent: "God is not a human being." How then can the man Jesus, who repeatedly spoke of God in the third person, possess divine attributes or be called without qualification, as in John 1:1, "God"?

When British naturalists first read accounts of the platypus, they were inclined to think that the reporters had been victims of a hoax, and when the first dried pelt made it to England, the scientists looked for stitches, convinced that the specimen could not be authentic. The platypus has a beak and lays eggs, so it should be a bird. But it also has fur, is warm-blooded, and suckles its young, so it should be a mammal. But it is additionally a monotreme — which means it has one exit for its urinary and intestinal systems — so it should be a reptile. In other words, the platypus has characteristics belonging to more than one species. We understand why some experts thought it must be bogus. The biologists eventually agreed to classify the platypus as a weird mammal. They could just as sensibly have decided to categorize it as a weird reptile or a weird bird, or they could have dubbed it the sole member of a brand new species.

What happens when a thing, let us dub it X, appears to possess characteristics of both A and B, and yet A and B are incompatible or mutually exclusive? There seem to be several options:

- X is A but not B (X only seems to be B).
- X is B but not A (X only seems to be A).

- X was A but then became B (or vice versa).
- X is a hybrid, part A and part B.
- X is neither A nor B but a third thing, C, with features of both A and B.
- X is paradoxically or mysteriously both A and B at the same time

The old christological debates, generated by the seemingly incompatible data, saw people making each one of these logical moves. The Ebionites, Jewish Christians who accepted Jesus as the Messiah, made him out to be a man, not God. They accordingly rejected traditions that did not fit this point of view (A not B). The docetists and Gnostics, to the contrary, eliminated the data which make Jesus human; they turned him into a divinity who only appeared to have had a body and who did not die (B not A). The so-called "dynamic monarchians" harmonized the conflicting traditions by arguing that the divine Word descended upon the human being Jesus, who at his baptism or resurrection was adopted into the Godhead (A became B). Apollinarians held that Jesus Christ had a human body and a human soul but not a human spirit, the reasonable divine Logos having replaced the latter (part A, part B). The Arians argued that the Son of God was the firstborn of creation, a sort of intermediary between God the Father and humanity (not A or B but C). Finally, the so-called orthodox ended up defending a paradox: Jesus was wholly human and wholly divine (both A and B).

Whether one approves or disapproves, the last solution, the orthodox solution, has dominated Christian theological history. But when one looks at how its advocates have, from ancient times, interpreted certain New Testament texts, one must object, at least if one has been trained to think historically. Again and again Jesus' deity has all but liquidated his humanity, making him a historically impossible figure. He has been a simulacrum, his humanity merely a doctrine to be believed, not a fact to be felt.

Let me illustrate with a few examples, the first being Matt. 24:36 and Mark 13:32, where the speaker denies his knowledge of the date of the consummation: "But about that day or hour no one knows, neither the angels of heaven, nor the Son, but only the Father."

Although the meaning of this sentence seems straightforward enough, the annals of theological exegesis, driven to uphold the equal dignity of Father and Son, are strewn with farfetched suggestions for making it say something else. The great Origen, like Gregory the Great after him, observed that the church is the body of Christ and then wondered whether Jesus might not be referring to the ignorance of Christians. Bishop Ambrose of Milan, so admired by Augustine, attributed "nor the son" to an Arian interpolation. Gregory Nazianzen, an important figure in the conquest of Arianism, offered that Jesus knew the eschatological date in his divine nature but not in his human nature. Ephrem the Syrian, overindulging his imagination, said that Jesus did not want to be pestered by people who thought he knew the time of the second coming, so he told a white lie, declaring that he did not know when he really did. Cassiodorus, the sixth-century Roman monk, contended, like Augustine before him, that "I do not know" really meant "I have not made you to know."[1] How could the judge of the last day not know when his own court would be in session?

If these readings now seem tendentious to today's New Testament scholars, this is due in part to the quest of the historical Jesus, which has promoted an unprecedented interpretive freedom and instilled a more realistic sense of the past. It has accomplished what the exegetical arguments of the Arians, Socinians, and Unitarians, who rightly insisted that Matt. 24:36 = Mark 13:32 subordinates the Son to the Father, were unable to accomplish.

Biblical scholars now engage in autonomous historical work, paying heed to the principle of historical plausibility as well as to their theological tradition; or perhaps they disregard theology altogether and try to conduct themselves simply as diligent historians. In either case, they are now fully aware that fourth-century Christian theology cannot be identified with first-century Christian theology. And in the present case, given what we now know about the development of Christian doctrine, the comments of Origen, Ambrose, and the others on Matt. 24:36 = Mark 13:32 must be regarded as defensive exegesis, as special pleading. The church fathers read the logion with presuppositions foreign to it, presuppositions that indeed contradict it. They found only what they wanted to find, reading their own christology into the Gospels so that Jesus might hand it right back to them.

Another example of christological dogma cultivating tendentious

---

1. Origen, *Commentary on Matthew* Latin 55; Ambrose, *On the Faith, to Gratian* 5.16.193; Gregory Nazianzen, *Oration 30* 15; Ephrem the Syrian, *Commentary on the Diatessaron* 18.16; Cassiodorus, *Exposition on the Psalms* on 9:39.

exegesis appears in the ecclesiastical commentaries on Matt. 20:23 and Mark 10:39-40. The saying, in its Matthean version, reads: "He said to them, 'You will indeed drink my cup, and you will be baptized with the baptism with which I am baptized; but to sit at my right hand, and at my left, is not mine to give; but it shall fall to those for whom it is prepared by my Father.'" Christian commentators, insisting on the parity among the members of the Trinity, have done their best to undo the plain sense of the sacred text. Chrysostom, citing Matt. 16:19, where Jesus gives Peter the keys to the kingdom, and 2 Tim. 4:8, where Jesus will give Paul a crown at the end, affirmed that Jesus has the power that he here denies having. Calvin went in the same direction: "By this reply Christ surrenders nothing. . . . He does not here reason as to his power, but only desires us to consider for what purpose he was sent by the Father, and what corresponds to his calling, and therefore distinguishes between the secret purpose of God and the nature of that teaching which had been enjoined on him." These words are convoluted because the biblical text defies Calvin's beliefs. Neither did the text sanction the theology of the exegete Bengel, who wrote: "Jesus does not say that it is not His to give . . . but defines and declares to whom He will give it, and the time and order, referring all to the Father, as usual."[2] But, incontrovertibly, Jesus does "say that it is not His to give." Something has gone awry here.

Our theological tradition is full of tendentious, ahistorical readings of Gospel texts, readings that have served orthodox christological agendas instead of historical truth. The Venerable Bede, following an exegetical tradition whose chief proponent was Cyril of Alexandria, took Luke 2:52 ("Jesus increased in wisdom and in years") to mean that Jesus advanced in wisdom, not by accruing over time "what he did not have, but by making available to others the gift of grace that he already possessed." Gregory the Great, sounding like so many others, said that, when Satan met Jesus in the desert (Matt. 4:1-11; Mark 1:12-13; Luke 4:1-13), the latter was tempted "outwardly," that is, in appearance only; "inwardly," his soul "rested in his divinity" and "remained unshaken." According to Clement of Alexandria, "It would be ridiculous to imagine that the body of the redeemer, in order to exist, had the usual needs of a human being.

---

2. Chrysostom, *Commentary on Matthew* 65.3; John Calvin, *A Harmony of the Gospels Matthew, Mark and Luke*, vol. 2 (Grand Rapids, MI: Eerdmans, 1972), p. 273; Johann Albrecht Bengel, *Gnomon Novi Testamentii* (2 vols.; Tübingen: Ludov. Frid. Fues, 1850), 1:49.

He only took food and ate it in order that we should not teach about him in a docetic fashion." Theophylact thought it possible that, when Jesus cried out, "My God, my God, why have you forsaken me?" (Matt. 27:46; Mark 15:34), he was speaking not for himself but on behalf of others: "Why have you forsaken the Jewish race, O Father, that it should commit such a sin and be handed over to destruction? For as Christ was one of the Jews, he said, 'forsaken me,' meaning, 'Why have you forsaken my kinsmen, my people, that they should bring such a great evil upon themselves?'" Thomas Aquinas found himself wondering why Jesus, being himself the omnipotent God, prayed.[3]

It is impossible, after immersing oneself in the quest for the historical Jesus, with its obligation to set the traditions about Jesus within their first-century contexts, to take any of this seriously as history — and Christians belonging to more conservative churches should find this disturbing. For the theologians and exegetes I have quoted are not from the margins of ecclesiastical history; they are rather, every one of them, important figures, even classical authorities. Furthermore, they represent mainstream christological dogma, the tradition that led to and flowed from Nicea. What then does it mean that, until relatively recent times, our dominant theologians have put Jesus into a christological straitjacket, that they have, despite their protests otherwise, been docetists of a sort, for whom Jesus' humanity was above all a philosophical problem? And what should we think when we learn that those theologians defended their christological opinions primarily by appeal to biblical texts, and yet again and again misconstrued or distorted texts having to do with Jesus' identity?

Unmasking defensive, tendentious, unhistorical exegesis conducted on behalf of traditional christology is not the only problem the quest hands those of us in the creedal churches. Is it in truth theologically inconsequential that John's Gospel, "the major battlefield in the New Testament during the Arian controversy,"[4] is today little used as a source for the historical Jesus? Does it matter that the long discourses in John, which contain the New Testament's highest christology, have been, be-

3. Bede, *Homilies on the Gospels* 1.19 (cf. Anselm, *Why Did God Become Man?* 1.9); Gregory the Great, *Moralia on Job* 3.16.29; Clement of Alexandria, *Stromata* 6.9; Theophylact, *Commentary on Matthew* ad loc.; Thomas Aquinas, *Summa Theologica* II.21.

4. R. P. C. Hanson, *The Search for the Christian Doctrine of God: The Arian Controversy 318-381* (Edinburgh: T. & T. Clark, 1988), p. 834.

ginning with Strauss, recognized by many scholars to come not from Jesus himself but to be instead Christian meditations from the end of the first century? Is it not a serious defect when Pope Benedict XVI, in his book on Jesus, allows the image of Jesus in John's Gospel to dominate his *historical* reconstruction?[5] Do not the words "Jesus Christ" change or lose at least some of their meaning when one ceases to imagine him composing the so-called high priestly prayer (John 17) or saying, "I am the way, the truth, and the life" (John 14:6)? Again, what does it mean that today's historians debate whether Jesus thought he was Messiah or what he meant by "the Son of man" but rarely if ever inquire into his awareness of having preexisted or into his consciousness of being the second member of the Trinity?

Some of my divinity students, who find themselves threatened by the discourse of the quest, the chief categories of which derive not from Christian theology but from the modern study of first-century Judaism, often wish that books on the historical Jesus would attribute to their Lord a higher christology, one more in accord with the faith in which they grew up. But their wish is vain, and they often end up fretting that Jesus might turn out to be like other important figures whose reputations among adherents exploded into myth after they were gone.

The reverent imaginations of some Jews bestowed omniscience upon Moses and gave him a seat in the heavens. In Mahayana Buddhism, the proclaimer became the proclaimed when some adherents identified Gautama with the absolute, deathless reality beyond all things. More to the point, Matthew amended Mark to advance a higher christology, and ideological tinkering must have gone on from the start. The questions all this raises are obvious.

If those in the more orthodox camps typically find the quest discouraging because it delivers a Jesus with a non-Nicene christology and even raises the specter of unwarranted ecclesiastical embellishment, others are perhaps anxious that he might have had too high a christology. These are the modern-day counterparts of the old Ebionites. Partly in reaction to an orthodox tradition that has done injustice to Jesus' humanity, these Christians steadfastly maintain that Jesus was truly one of us (A not B). They dismiss his deification or reinterpret it in something other than on-

5. Pope Benedict XVI, *Jesus of Nazareth: From the Baptism in the Jordan to the Transfiguration* (Garden City, NY: Doubleday, 2007).

tological terms. To confess Jesus' divinity is, on this view, to speak the language of love and devotion, not the language of philosophy. Calling him "very God of very God" is mythology, not metaphysics, poetry, not prose, a hymn of commitment, not an ontological proposition. Jesus is God for us, or a picture of what God is like, or our god as opposed to any other god. But he is not, in and of himself, the Lord God.[6]

Those who adopt this position are not driven to discover that Jesus had a high christology, and they may even find such a prospect embarrassing. If, for instance, one wishes Jesus to remain an inspiring figure and yet does not believe that he will someday return to judge the world, what is the attraction in supposing that he entertained such a stupendous thought about himself? Some may even wonder about the mental health of the man in the Gospels, who makes so many exalted, egocentric statements about himself, especially in his eschatological forecasts. Both Albert Schweitzer (in 1911) and Walter Bundy (in 1922) wrote entire books documenting the opinion of some that Jesus must have been "eccentric," a "braggart" and a "fanatic," perhaps "insane."[7]

Such worries are still with us. According to the late New Testament scholar John Knox, anyone who identified himself with the returning Son of man must have had "serious psychological difficulties." Knox was unable to "imagine a sane human being, of any historical period or culture, entertaining the thoughts about himself which the Gospels, as they stand, often attribute to" their main character.[8] It comes as no surprise to learn that Knox, an ordained Episcopalian who instructed divinity students, did not assign such thoughts to Jesus himself; he thereby avoided the implicit diagnosis of mental illness. More recently, Marcus Borg has written this:

If you think you are the light of the world, you're not. That is, perceiving oneself in such grand terms is a fairly good indicator that you're off base. The parallel statement, of course, is: if you think

6. For a clear, representative statement see John Hick, *The Metaphor of God Incarnate: Christology in a Pluralistic Age* (2nd ed.; Louisville, KY: Westminster/John Knox, 2006).

7. Albert Schweitzer, *The Psychiatric Study of Jesus: Exposition and Criticism* (Boston: Beacon, 1948); Walter E. Bundy, *The Psychic Health of Jesus* (New York: Macmillan, 1922).

8. John Knox, *The Death of Christ: The Cross in New Testament History and Faith* (New York/Nashville: Abingdon, 1958), pp. 58, 71.

you are the messiah, you're not. . . . Though saints and Spirit persons are a bit crazy, when judged by conventional standards, they typically do not think of themselves in grandiose terms. I don't think people like Jesus have an exalted perception of themselves.[9]

These are refreshingly candid words, even if they are, in my judgment, more than incautious. For Borg, a historical Jesus with too high a christology, indeed a Jesus with only a Synoptic christology, would be not an asset but a liability.

I strongly suspect that Borg's sentiment is shared by others working in the field of New Testament studies and further that such feeling has affected their views about Jesus. I cannot, admittedly, confirm this suspicion, because most academics are not as self-revealing as Borg. Be that fact as it may, Martin Hengel has documented the aversion, arising from ideological factors, of several twentieth-century German scholars to the notion that Jesus imagined himself to be Messiah.[10] It seems, then, that granting to Jesus too high a christology is, for some, just as unwelcome as a low christology is to the more orthodox.

Surprisingly perhaps, the historical facts are no more congenial to the former than to the latter. This is because Borg is almost certainly wrong. Jesus, we have good reason to believe, did indeed have an exalted self-conception, even if it was not the conception of Nicea.

Others will, of course, disagree with my evaluation that Jesus made himself out to be somebody: those involved in the quest for the historical Jesus speak with many voices on this subject. But, as already observed on pp. 64-66, Jesus' starring role in the eschatological drama is all over the sources, in words attributed to him and in words assigned to others, in stories as well as in sayings. Funk's proposition that "Jesus had nothing to say about himself, other than that he had no permanent address, no bed to sleep in, no respect on his home turf"[11] contradicts the broad testimony of the relevant sources. It also, beyond that, has the disadvantage of making it much harder to explain the lofty evaluation of Jesus in pre-Pauline tradition.

9. Marcus Borg, "Was Jesus God?," in *The Meaning of Jesus: Two Visions*, by Marcus Borg and N. T. Wright (San Francisco: HarperSanFrancisco, 1999), pp. 146-47.

10. Martin Hengel, *Studies in Early Christology* (Edinburgh: T&T Clark, 1995), pp. 1-72.

11. Robert W. Funk, *Honest to Jesus: Jesus for a New Millennium* (San Francisco: HarperSanFrancisco, 1996), p. 41.

Reconstructing, as has Funk, a Jesus who "had nothing to say about himself" presumes that, although our chief informants are mistaken in the impression they leave, we can know better, that we can know that he did not take himself to be, or to be destined to be, Israel's eschatological redeemer. No one, however, has the sleuthing ability to subtract with razor-like precision the ecclesiastical accretions, read between the remaining lines, and discover that the historical truth was nearly the opposite of what we find in Matthew, Mark, and Luke. If the extant sources are as misleading as Funk's evaluation implies, then surely the safe and sensible position would be agnosticism. But the safest and most sensible bet of all is that the Roman authorities executed Jesus as a royal claimant — "king of the Jews" — precisely because some people thought of him as such, and he did not repudiate them.

I will not, in this context, rehearse further the arguments that, taken together, imply that Jesus regarded himself as the central figure in the eschatological drama. My point here instead is that I have said enough to indicate that his apparent self-perception, if granted, should pose questions all around. Those who subscribe to Nicea should be anxious, for the historical Jesus did not think of himself what they think of him. To be sure, his identity, like that of the rest of us, cannot be restricted to his self-conscious evaluation, whatever we judge that to have been. Jesus must be more than the sum of his own thoughts. Still, traditional, orthodox christologies have assumed that Jesus was fully aware of his own godhead and spoke accordingly, whereas modern criticism has, in the judgment of many of us, exterminated this possibility. The orthodox tradition thus needs to acknowledge that the revisionist christologies of the last two centuries have been partly occasioned by advances in knowledge. There has been good cause to rethink some things.

As for those who reject or radically reinterpret Nicea and Chalcedon, a historical Jesus who placed himself at the center of a mythological endtime scenario is not likely to be regarded with affection. For such an individual conceived himself to be extraordinary and indeed unique, in a category all his own. As with the orthodox, so too, then, with their opponents: their evaluation of Jesus does not line up with his evaluation of himself.

The upshot of the foregoing pages is that the historical Jesus remains, in Schweitzer's familiar words, a stranger and an enigma. As a Christian, however, I do not find this so dreadful. What good is Jesus if he does not trouble our theological dreams? Certainly the character in the

Gospels combats complacency and self-satisfaction, and what but complacency and self-satisfaction can come from a historical Jesus who confirms us in our theological ways, whether those ways be liberal or conservative? A domesticated Jesus who sounds like us, makes us comfortable, and commends our opinions is no Jesus at all.

Eschatology: Here to Stay

The matter of Jesus' own christology cannot be disentangled from his eschatological expectations, for in the Synoptics it is chiefly in logia about the last things that his status is most exalted. In Matt. 10:32-33 = Luke 12:8-9, confession or denial of Jesus correlates with being confessed or denied at the final assize. In Matt. 11:2-5 = Luke 7:18-23, Jesus implicitly identifies himself with the eschatological figure John the Baptist foretold — "the coming one" who will baptize with fire (cf. Matt. 3:11-12 = Luke 3:16-17). In Mark 14:62, Jesus is the Danielic "Son of man" who will come on the clouds of heaven.

Modern scholarship has busied itself with the origin and meaning of these and the other eschatological prophecies in the Gospels. Driving much of this effort has been the troubling business of whether Jesus' expectations were disappointed. To abbreviate an oft-told story:

Most Christians have traditionally thought that, when he announced the near arrival of the kingdom of God, Jesus had in view the new age of the church. He also, they have believed, foresaw in the offing Easter, Pentecost, and the destruction of Jerusalem. By contrast, his speech about the final judgment posited an event in the chronological distance.

Reimarus, when biblical criticism was still in its cradle in the eighteenth century, rid himself of these conventional ideas, arguing instead, on the basis of Jewish rather than ecclesiastical sources, that Jesus envisioned an earthly kingdom in Jerusalem, with himself on the throne, a kingdom that would rout the Romans and make real the paradisical oracles of the Old Testament. Because none of this transpired, the disciples invented the second coming.

Reimarus did not win a large fan base. Nor, in the nineteenth century, did Strauss, who urged that, if Jesus sincerely foretold his own second coming on the clouds of heaven, then we must dismiss him as a fanatic. More successful at persuasion was Johannes Weiss, whose careful exegetical work convinced many that, when Jesus proclaimed the kingdom of God, he was heralding the end time brought about by God, not the progressive realization of social justice through religious idealism. Among the converts was Schweitzer, who enthusiastically endorsed Weiss's contribution, which he turned into the prequel to his own presentation of a thoroughly eschatological Jesus.

Much of twentieth-century scholarship has offered variations on Weiss and Schweitzer. Bultmann and Jeremias, for instance, endorsed the proposal that Jesus was an apocalyptic prophet, even if (with good reason) they dispensed with many of the particulars of Schweitzer's imaginative reconstruction. Cullmann and Werner Kümmel also largely fell in line, although both urged that Jesus expected an interim period between his death and the eschatological finale.

But not all have gone along. Indeed, the study of Jesus and apocalyptic has turned into a series of battles without truce for over a hundred years now. Few seem nonchalant about the matter.

Many, disconcerted by the errant Jesus of Weiss and Schweitzer, have resisted the force of their arguments. Dodd ingeniously read the Synoptic texts so that they give us "realized eschatology": the kingdom had already come in Jesus' ministry. Crossan, segregating Jesus from a very large number of traditions about him, has him reject the violent expectations of the Baptist and instead hope for a utopian future of justice and egalitarianism, a future occasioned not by the last judgment but by social renewal. Tom Wright passionately promotes a Jesus who used eschatological metaphors to prophesy what in fact came to pass in the first century — his own resurrection, the ecclesia, Jerusalem's violent demise. When Jesus spoke of the Son of man coming on the clouds of heaven, he was not fantasizing about a sky ride on condensed vapors but was being poetic. He meant that the clouds of judgment were gathering.

Not one of these eloquent appeals suffices to overthrow the common verdict: whether we like it or not, the historical Jesus was the apocalyptic Jesus. Having elsewhere shared my several reasons for taking this view of the matter, for deciding that the shared hypothesis of Weiss and Schweitzer is not just tenable but compelling, I need not repeat myself here.[12] What I do wish to underscore before continuing is that positing

---

12. See especially Dale C. Allison, Jr., *Constructing Jesus: Memory and Imagination* (Grand Rapids, MI: Baker Academic, 2009).

an apocalyptic Jesus coheres with the critical method introduced earlier in this volume, a method which proceeds not by interpreting supposedly authenticated traditions but rather by making inferences from patterns that characterize the sources as a whole. Consider the following list of observations, whose length should trouble those who wish to bid farewell to Weiss and Schweitzer:

- A few logia declare that the sands of ordinary time have almost run out: Mark 9:1; 13:30; Matt. 10:23 (cf. Luke 18:8: "he will vindicate them speedily").
- The same temporal conviction appears in Matt. 23:34-35 = Luke 11:49-51, which declares that all blood shed from the foundation of the world will be "required of this generation." In order for this to make sense, "this generation" must be the last generation.
- "The day of judgment" and its abbreviated stand-ins "the judgment" and "that day" envisage the eschatological assize: Matt. 10:15 = Luke 10:12; Matt. 11:22, 24; 12:36; Luke 10:14.
- Luke 12:5 = Matt. 10:28; Mark 9:43-45 (cf. Matt. 18:8-9); and Matt. 5:22; 23:15, 33 refer specifically to Gehenna, the antithesis of heaven, the frightful place of postmortem or eschatological punishment.
- That place of punishment is depicted as a place of fire in Matt. 7:19; Mark 9:47-48; Luke 12:49; John 15:6 (and perhaps Mark 9:49), as often in Jewish apocalyptic texts.
- Matt. 18:6-7 = Luke 17:1-2 and Mark 9:42 warn that the punishment for harming others will be worse than having a millstone around the neck and being thrown into the sea. Only the eschatological judgment could impose a fate worse than that.
- Matt. 22:13 and 25:30 speak of "the outer darkness."
- Matt. 24:51 refers to "the weeping and gnashing of teeth."
- As it appears in Matt. 24:45-51 and Luke 12:42-46, the parable of the unfaithful slave functions as a warning about the coming judgment.
- The enigmatic Matt. 24:40-41 = Luke 17:34-35 (cf. *Gospel of Thomas* 61), about one being taken and another left, means either that the wicked will be plucked from the earth (cf. Matt. 13:41) or (more likely) that the righteous will be taken to meet the Son of man in the air (cf. Mark 13:27; 1 Thess. 4:17). Whatever option is correct, the final judgment coincides with a supernatural sorting.
- Luke 17:26-30 (cf. Matt. 24:37-39) likens the coming judgment to

Noah's flood and sulfur falling upon Sodom, both events being, in Jewish and Christian literature, popular prototypes of the last judgment and end of the world.

- Matt. 13:36-43 interprets Matt. 13:24-30 (= *Gospel of Thomas* 57) as an allegory of the division of just and unjust on the final day.
- Matt. 13:47-50, the parable of the net, depicts the same division under a different figure.
- Matt. 25:31-46 presents a memorable picture of the great judgment, introduced by the simile of a shepherd separating sheep from goats.
- The threat of eschatological judgment has its counterpart in the promise of heavenly or everlasting reward: Matt. 5:12 = Luke 6:23; Mark 10:29-30; Matt. 5:19; John 6:40; 14:2-3; *Gospel of Thomas* 19, 114.
- The tale of the rich man and Lazarus in Luke 16:19-31 promotes humanitarian conduct by depicting pleasant reward in "Abraham's bosom" and miserable retribution in "Hades."
- The paradoxical sayings about reversal in status — the first will be last, the last first, etc. — are not naively optimistic observations about everyday human experience (Matt. 10:39 = Luke 17:33; Matt. 23:12 = Luke 14:11; Matt. 25:29 = Luke 19:26; Mark 4:25; 8:35; 10:31; Matt. 13:12; Luke 18:14; *Gospel of Thomas* 4). This is why they use the future tense — "will be exalted," "will keep it [life]," "will be first." They foresee God turning the world upside down, which can only be the result of the coming judgment.
- In view of the parallel in the Kaddish ("May he let his kingdom rule in your lifetime and in your days and in the lifetime of the whole house of Israel, speedily and soon") and the associations that "kingdom" often has in ancient Palestinian Jewish literature, "your kingdom come" (Matt. 6:10 = Luke 11:2) is more likely than not a prayer for God to redeem the world once and for all.
- Mark 1:15; Matt. 12:28 = Luke 11:20; and 22:18 attach temporal verbs to "kingdom" (e.g., Matt. 10:7 = Luke 10:9). They thereby advert not to a changeless reality but rather to the dramatic advent of an unprecedented, supernatural reality. In these sayings, "the kingdom of God" is nearly synonymous with "the age to come" or "the new creation."
- The futurity of the kingdom is also manifest in the sayings about entering it (Mark 10:15, 23-25; Matt. 5:20; 7:21; 23:13). The future tense in Mark 10:23 and Matt. 5:20, the parallelism in Mark 9:43-47 ("into life" = "into the kingdom"), the eschatological sense of passing through

the narrow door or gate in Matt. 7:13 = Luke 13:24, and the circumstance that it is not the kingdom that enters people but people who
enter the kingdom all make the meaning plain enough: the saints
will, at the end of days, cross the threshold into a redeemed world.

- The Jesus of Mark 10:30 invokes the distinction, known from the rabbis, between "this age" and "the age to come."
- Some logia about the Son of man clearly allude to the scene of the
last judgment in Daniel 7: Mark 13:26; 14:62; Matt. 10:32-33 = Luke
12:8-9; Matt. 19:28 = Luke 22:28-30; John 5:27.
- The canonical Jesus believes in the resurrection of the dead: Mark
12:18-27; Matt. 12:41-42 = Luke 11:31-32; Luke 14:12-14; John 5:28-29.
- The belief that unprecedented tribulation will herald the advent of
the new age and that the kingdom of Satan will not go away without
a fight, appears not only in Mark 13:3-23 but also in Matt. 11:12-13 =
Luke 16:16 (the kingdom now suffers violence) and Matt. 10:34-36 =
Luke 12:51-53 (cf. *Gospel of Thomas* 16; it is the time not of peace but
of the sword).
- Several times Jesus admonishes people to be on the alert because
the eschatological crisis may come at any time: Matt. 24:43-51 = Luke
12:39-46; Mark 13:33-37; Matt. 25:1-13; Luke 12:35-38; 21:34-36.
- Mark 14:25 and Luke 14:24; 22:30 look forward to the eschatological
banquet.
- Jesus has twelve disciples, their number being that of the tribes of Israel. This circumstance almost certainly reflects the common expectation, with roots in Jeremiah and Ezekiel, that, at the end of
days, all twelve tribes would return to the land. The twelve are a symbolic representation of restored Israel. In line with this, Matt. 19:28 =
Luke 22:28-30 promises some of Jesus' followers that they will
"judge" — which means either "rule" or "pass judgment upon" — the
twelve tribes of Israel. The return of the scattered from the Diaspora
is also the subject of Matt. 8:11-12 = Luke 13:28-29, for the "many" who
come "from east and west" and are hosted by the patriarchs, Abraham, Isaac, and Jacob, must include the scattered tribes.
- Some texts depict Jesus as "the Messiah," an end-time deliverer:
Mark 8:27-30; 11:9-10; Matt. 23:10; John 1:41; 4:25, 29; 6:14-15; 9:22; 10:24;
11:27 (cf. Mark 15:2, 9, 18, 26, 32).
- The canonical Jesus regards eschatological oracles in the Hebrew Bible as being fulfilled in his own time; see Matt. 11:10 = Luke 7:27, citing

Mal. 3:1; Mark 9:13, adverting to Mal. 4:5-6; Mark 14:27, quoting Zech. 13:7; and Matt. 5:17, asserting in general that Jesus fulfills "the law and the prophets."

- Jesus, responding to a query from John the Baptist, implicitly equates himself with the latter's "coming one" (Matt. 11:2-5 = Luke 7:18-23), an eschatological judge (Matt. 3:11-12 = Luke 7:16-17). He does this by taking up the language of prophetic texts in Isaiah (26:19; 29:18-19; 35:5-6; 42:18; 61:1), implying that he is their fulfillment. The beatitudes, where Jesus comforts those who mourn (Matt. 5:3, 4, 6, 11-12 = Luke 6:20-23), do something similar inasmuch as they too echo Isaiah 61; and Luke 4:16-19 has Jesus reading from Isaiah 61 and finding its prophecies fulfilled in his ministry.
- Luke 19:11 says that, when Jesus neared Jerusalem, his disciples "supposed that the kingdom of God was to appear immediately"; and John 21:20-23 (discussed below) reflects the belief of some Christians that Jesus promised the end during the lifetime of his disciples.

I do not contend, because I do not believe, that all this material comes from Jesus, directly or indirectly. Nor do I insist that any of it is word-perfect memory. To repeat what I have said before: the Synoptics are not primarily records of what Jesus actually said and did but collections of impressions. They recount, or rather often recount, the sorts of things that he said and did, or that he could have said and done. As for eschatology in particular, my contention is that either a decent number of the entries in my catalogue fairly characterize what Jesus was about, or the tradition is so full of mnemonic holes and fictional accretions that the quest is a vain aspiration and we should find some other pastime with which to amuse ourselves.

Opting, as I do, for the former alternative entails that Jesus had firm eschatological expectations, to which he gave frequent expression. More precisely, he envisaged, as did many in his time and place, the advent, after suffering and persecution, of a great judgment, and after that a supernatural utopia, the kingdom of God, inhabited by the dead come back to life, to enjoy a world forever rid of evil and wholly ruled by God. Further, he thought that the night was far gone, the day at hand.

This is not to say that Jesus had only eschatology on his mind. Although I once subscribed to and publicly defended Schweitzer's "thorough-going eschatology," I do so no longer. I suppose I was the victim of system-mongering, of the rationalistic impulse to make all the pieces of the tradition fit snugly together without remainder. I have come to see that too much associates itself only obliquely, if at all, with eschatology, that the puzzle will always have large lacunae, and that we will always be left with pieces that go nowhere. Nonetheless, Jesus did, when gazing about, perceive a perishing world, and in accord with then-contemporary readings of the prophetic oracles of the Hebrew Scriptures, he hoped for a re-created world, a heaven on earth, a paradise liberated from devils and illness. And this was for him no vague inkling or tangential thought but a consuming hope.

His dream, however, has remained a dream. It is not just that, as Matt. 24:36 = Mark 13:32 says, the Son had no knowledge of precisely when the end would come. It is rather that the Son expected and encouraged others to expect that all would wrap up soon, and yet run-of-the-mill history remains with us: Satan still goes to and fro upon the earth.

Most Christians cannot abide an errant Jesus. In 1907, Pope Pius X rebuked a collection of modernist errors, among which was the following: "Everyone who is not led by preconceived opinions can readily see that . . . Jesus professed an error concerning the immediate Messianic coming." The Holy Office, in condemning this historical judgment, here assumes that a Jesus with a near expectation discredits the Roman Catholic religion. Even those without any residual fundamentalism have often resisted a fallible, apocalyptic Jesus, and the time since Schweitzer has witnessed any number of tactics for shunning him.

Just how desperate the arguments have sometimes become is cogently illustrated by the strategy of the Very Reverend H. Erskine Hill, who in 1916 published a book entitled *Apocalyptic Problems*. Irritated that "some ordinarily cautious and conservative writers have come to assume that the Christ Himself entertained an expectation that failed," and confidently insisting that "mystical insight" is a better guide than "mere scholarship," Hill wrote these astounding words: Jesus'

> sayings were constantly misinterpreted even by His Apostles, and He knew that they were misunderstood and left them unexplained. . . . He left them as unintelligible as books are to babies, waiting until man should be sufficiently developed to understand them. . . . He spoke for all ages and His words can wait the development of the spiritual faculties by the aid of which alone they

can be understood. From this point of view the popular opinions which prevailed in the primitive Church would seem to be comparatively unimportant as an aid to interpretation.[13]

This statement concedes that the Apostles and the primitive Church expected an imminent and spectacular parousia, but only because they got Jesus wrong. We, Hill avows, with our improved spiritual perception, can now get him right. We may happily dismiss, then, the execrable Jesus of imminent expectation as an unfortunate misunderstanding, which a patient, far-sighted Jesus did nothing to counter. Nothing is amiss.

I need not document further the cognitive dissonance of people who, preferring their theological inclinations to the historical facts, mistreat our sources, thereby obtaining a Jesus more to their liking. Not all the strategies are as lame as that of Hill, whom to quote is to refute. Many of those who have supplied alternatives to Weiss and Schweitzer have taught us much. In the end, however, their reconstructions have all failed, just like Jesus' expectations.

So how should we respond? The widespread dismay arises in part, I submit, from a failure to comprehend fully that eschatological language does not give us a preview of coming events but is rather, as the study of comparative religion teaches us, religious hope in mythological dress. Narratives about the unborn future are fictions, in the same way that narratives about the creation of the world are fictions.

The end is like the beginning. Genesis is no historical record of the primordial past, and the New Testament offers no precognitive history of the eschatological future. The New Jerusalem, the last judgment, and the resurrection are, just like Eden, the serpent, and Adam, theological parables. We must interpret them not literally but as religious poetry, which means with our theologically-informed imaginations. They are visions of the future in precisely the same way as are the parable of the ten virgins and the parable of the weeds and the wheat; that is, they are symbolic figures of what eye has not seen or ear heard and so can only be imagined. Luther says somewhere that we know no more of the new world awaiting us than a babe in its mother's womb knows of the world into which it is about to be born. Given this, all we can do is what Jesus and the early

---

13. H. Erskine Hill, *Apocalyptic Problems* (London/New York/Toronto: Hodder and Stoughton, 1916), pp. 15-17.

Christians did: project present religious experience and faith and theological reflection onto the longed-for future — just as the authors of Genesis projected their religious experience and faith and theological reflection onto the imagined past.

How does all this bear on the vexed subject of imminent eschatology? It matters not, once we understand Genesis aright, what year the book implicitly sets for the world's first dawn. Bishop Ussher's calculation of 4004 BC must be wrong because the series of events he ostensibly dated never took place. The calendar is irrelevant, for no woman ever came forth from a man's rib, and God never called the light day. So nobody's calculation of creation's day, month, or year could ever be correct, just as nobody's localization of the fictional Eden — a place that was never on the map — could ever be correct.

In like fashion, locating the coming of the Son of man in the distant future is no more sensible than locating the occasion in the near future: mythological events do not intersect the historical time line. The parousia is a parable, a projection of the mythopoeic imagination. Its date cannot be known because it has no date.

Most religious traditions have eschatological beliefs. Such beliefs often remain in the background, remain doctrines about the by-and-by that do not much inform or impinge on the present. Imminent eschatological expectation, whenever it makes its appearance, moves those doctrines to center stage. It activates, for those who live with the requisite beliefs, their myths of the last things, making them urgently germane. Proclaiming a near end confronts people with a decision that cannot wait. In addition, because such proclamation typically arises among the disenfranchised, it can rudely unmask the sins of the status quo, thus bringing to dramatic and needed expression the divine discontent with the world as it is, a world bad enough that it needs to be improved out of existence. It also fittingly enlarges hope in a transcendent Reality without which the dream of radically revising the present evil age seems doomed to failure and the establishing of everlasting justice and meaning unobtainable. With all of which I, as a Christian, more than sympathize. As B. H. Streeter wrote almost a century ago:

> The summits of certain mountains are seen only at rare moments
> when, their cloud-cap rolled away, they stand out stark and clear.
> So in ordinary life ultimate values and eternal issues are normally

obscured by minor duties, petty cares, and small ambitions; at the bedside of a dying man the cloud is often lifted. In virtue of the eschatological hope our Lord and His first disciples found themselves standing, as it were, at the bedside of a dying world. Thus for a whole generation the cloud of lesser interests was rolled away, and ultimate values and eternal issues stood out before them stark and clear. . . . The majority of men in all ages best serve their kind by a life of quiet duty, in the family, in their daily work, and in the support of certain definite and limited public and philanthropic causes. . . . But it has been well for humanity that during one great epoch the belief that the end of all was near turned the thoughts of the highest minds away from practical and local interests, even of the first importance, like the condition of slaves in Capernaum or the sanitation of Tarsus.[14]

At this point, however, honesty compels us to acknowledge that any modern interpretation of eschatology as myth cannot be equated with the interpretation of Jesus, who was, after all, a first-century Jew. Although he often spoke in parables, I cannot say that he understood the last judgment and attendant events to be figurative in the same way that I do. An unbiased reading of the evidence informs us that the ancients in general and Jesus in particular took their eschatology much more literally than do many of us.[15] So here we must go our own way, without Jesus in the lead, just as we must go our own modern way in reinterpreting Genesis — and any number of other biblical texts — in opposition to the assumptions of our predecessors in the faith, including the biblical writers.

We are not, however, without any backing from tradition when we promote — for ourselves, not for Jesus — a less than literal interpretation of apocalyptic eschatology. John's Gospel gives us canonical precedent for this sort of hermeneutical move. While the book retains the

14. B. H. Streeter, "The Historic Christ," in *Foundations: A Statement of Christian Belief in Terms of Modern Thought: By Seven Oxford Men*, by B. H. Streeter, et al. (London: Macmillan, 1913), pp. 119-20.

15. See Dale C. Allison, Jr., "Jesus and the Victory of Apocalyptic," in *Jesus and the Restoration of Israel: A Critical Assessment of N. T. Wright's "Jesus and the Victory of God*," ed. Carey C. Newman (Downers Grove: Inter-Varsity, 1999), pp. 126-41, and Edward Adams, *The Stars Will Fall from Heaven: Cosmic Catastrophe in the New Testament and Its World* (London/New York: T. & T. Clark, 2007).

concept of a "last day," it nonetheless represents a fundamental rethinking of Christian existence. It replaces the eschatological speech of Matt. 24–25; Mark 13; and Luke 21 with the intimate words of encouragement at the Last Supper (John 13–17), which mostly omits apocalyptic expectations. Written when the delay of the parousia could be felt (cf. 2 Pet. 3:1-10), the Gospel prudently focuses not on Jesus coming on the clouds of heaven in the future but on the Spirit coming to believers in the present. It emphasizes not that the dead will someday rise (although it does not deny that) but rather that the living can even now enjoy eternal life. It teaches not the impending defeat of evil in a cosmic judgment but the routing of the devil at Jesus' crucifixion. It is almost as though the Evangelist systematically set out to translate the literal into the figurative, sought to reinterpret, in terms of present religious experience, the apocalyptic mythology he found in the Jesus tradition.

Even here, however, we must candidly acknowledge a hitch. The Gospel, at least in its canonical form, seems to deny what it is doing. It takes for granted, indeed asserts, that its thoughts are the thoughts of Jesus, and that its reinterpretation is really no reinterpretation at all.

This appears not only from the attribution of its inspired meditations to Jesus but also from the secondary addendum in ch. 21. Here Jesus asks Peter concerning the Beloved Disciple, "If it is my will that he remain until I come, what is that to you? Follow me!" This quotation explains, we are told, why "the rumor spread in the community that this disciple would not die." Yet the rumor is untrue: "Jesus did not say to him that he would not die but, 'If it is my will that he remain until I come, what is that to you?'" Obviously behind these verses is Christian anxiety: the Beloved Disciple had died but Jesus had not yet returned. Some saying such as Matt. 10:23 or Mark 9:1 or Mark 13:30, taken at face value, that is, understood to mean that not all of Jesus' disciples would die before the consummation, must lie in the background, and all the disciples must now be dead. John 21:22-23 responds by denying that Jesus ever said such a thing or that, if he did, he was misunderstood. But if following the quest has led us to an apocalyptic Jesus, we must, even if we find John's reinterpretation of the tradition hermeneutically instructive, respectfully disagree on this score with whoever wrote John 21. Jesus apparently did expect the coming of God sooner rather than later, and it is only natural that the passing of time witnessed, if not a far-flung crisis of faith, then at least some uneasiness here and there.

I do not expect even sympathetic readers to agree with everything in the foregoing pages. Eschatology is an unusually challenging topic, and there are no pat answers. But modern scholarship compels us to come up with something, for if the quest has produced an apocalyptic Jesus with a near expectation, then honoring him and the truth means coming to terms with that expectation. Anything else, however sophisticated or attractive, is escapism.

Context: Gone for Good

The quest of the historical Jesus should not only influence how we think about particular topics, such as christology and eschatology; it should also more generally alter how we appropriate each and every saying attributed to him.

Critical historiography has revealed that a high percentage of the logia of Jesus initially lacked a narrative context and that, later on, contexts were artificially created for them. The upshot is that we usually can only speculate about the original circumstances in which Jesus uttered any saying that we might assign to him.

The interpretive implications of this fact are both considerable and discouraging. For context bestows meaning, and if we do not know the context in which Jesus said this or that, then the riddle of what he meant may not be solvable.

My own view, as is clear from the previous chapter, is that we can still collect groups of sayings that are thematically related and interpret them in terms of what we otherwise know of Jesus' ministry and first-century Palestinian Judaism. Christians, however, have typically hankered after much more than this. They have wanted to know exactly what Jesus meant when he composed this aphorism or that parable. It is one thing to appeal to Matthew or Mark or Luke or John. It is quite another to have Jesus himself on one's side. But here the quest has humbled our ambition.

To illustrate: the followers of Jesus have, from early times, wondered whether his teachings permit them to go to war. The tendency of the pre-Constantinian churches was toward pacifism. The tendency of the post-Constantinian churches was away from it. Since the Reformation, the historic peace churches have kept the discussion before us. In doing so, they have repeatedly appealed to the Sermon on the Mount, above all to Matt. 5:38-48. They have thereby claimed Jesus for their cause. Did he not exhort us to turn the other cheek? Did he not command us to go the extra mile? Did he not instruct us to love our enemies? Was he not, then, a pacifist, like the Amish and Mennonites?

While the answers to these questions may seem obvious to some, they are not to me. The Sermon on the Mount is an extraordinarily difficult text to interpret, as the history of interpretation shows, and I remain uncertain as to how the Evangelist wanted readers to respond to Matt. 5:38-48. I am even more uncertain as to what Jesus himself might have intended by the sentiments collected in Matt. 5:38-48. The problem is that we do not know the occasion(s) for which he authored those sentiments. Perhaps he was speaking to his partners in ministry, to those who literally followed him around, and was giving them the sort of heroic instruction for itinerants that we find in the missionary discourses, instructions demanding the sacrifice of necessities. If doing without staff and money turned the disciples into walking parables, concrete displays of utter dependence on God, this might also have been the intended upshot of telling them to turn the other cheek, give away their cloaks, etc. But maybe Jesus was addressing sympathizers, or a crowd of Galilean villagers, in which case he might have intended a more general application.

The inescapable fact is that the original audience has dispersed, and we remain in the dark about its makeup, which means that we do not know exactly what Matt. 5:38-48 might have meant on Jesus' lips. Maybe his aim was large indeed. Maybe he was advancing principles of sufficient generality that they indict the use of all force and even implicitly raise questions about the militaristic stories we find in Joshua and Judges. Or maybe he was rather giving practical advice to peasants as to how to get along better in their villages, without any thoughts for the wider world or people going to war. Or maybe he was doing something else entirely. Whatever the truth, only God knows it.

Unfortunately, ignorance of Jesus' intent when composing a saying is, because we do not know the initial context(s), again and again our lot. If he warned that those who deny him will be denied at the last judgment, was he setting forth some sort of general soteriological principle? Or was he giving a word of exhortation to disciples sent out on mission, who might be tempted to abandon the cause when faced with hardship? When he prohibited divorce, was he rendering his verdict as to how all good Jews should act, or was he instead concerned that those in his immediate circle give no occasion for sexual scandal? If he forbade oaths, what sort of oaths did he have in mind? Was he thinking solely of private oaths in everyday life, or did he also have in view public oaths, the sort required by the courtroom?

To our everlasting frustration, we cannot respond with conviction to any of these important questions and dozens like them. Without knowing the real-life setting as opposed to the current literary context, the originating meaning is up for grabs. We can, to be sure, often profitably argue about what Matthew, Mark, Luke, or John wanted us to think, but Jesus is a much more difficult matter.

So here the outcome of the quest is negative. Among its lessons is our inability to know much that Christians have always wanted to know. This in turn entails a large dose of theological humility. We can still outline the general themes of Jesus' speech. But that we can, beyond that, fill in the details with robust confidence seems doubtful, however much we wish it were otherwise.

CHAPTER 5

Some Personal Impressions

"Meaning is a human category, and must be won against a background. A life that was inevitably meaningful would defeat itself from the start."

SUSAN NEIMAR

"How needful it is for me to enter into the darkness and to admit the coincidence of opposites, beyond all the grasp of reason, and there to seek the truth where impossibility meets me."

NICHOLAS OF CUSA

In this final chapter, I choose to concentrate on only three topics. I select them for personal reasons, because they have been and remain important to me. My silence about other matters, including matters that others might reckon more important or more central to their faith, should not be taken to imply that I deem them uninteresting or unimportant.[1]

---

1. I will not, in this chapter, attempt to justify my various assertions about the historical Jesus; in each case, however, I take myself to be arguing from recurrent themes and motifs.

Contradiction: Divine Love and Human Woe

God is, for Jesus, above all "Father," which is both a name and a meta-phor. This is striking. The chief theme in the tradition is the kingdom of God. We might expect, then, that its primary image of the divinity would be that of a king, especially as the image of God seated on a throne recurs so often in the Hebrew Bible and Judaism. References to God as king, however, appear only occasionally in the sources for Jesus, who far more frequently speaks of God as Father.

Partial explanation may lie in this, that Jesus and his hearers had no access to a royal court; that is, unlike weddings and fathers, lilies and the birds of the air, their firsthand knowledge of kings was nil. No less impor-tant than this social fact, however, is a theological fact: Jesus seems to have conceptualized the divine rule in contrast to the tyrannical rule of the stereotypical monarch.[2]

God does not, in the Jesus tradition, exploit human beings but re-lates to them in ways analogous to how a loving parent deals with a child. Instead of repressive dominion, there is care and nurture. Mark 10:42-43 censures pagan kings with these words: "You know that among the Gentiles those whom they recognize as their rulers lord it over them, and their great ones are tyrants over them. But it is not so among you; but whoever wishes to become great among you must be your servant." Rejection of oppressive lordship also appears in Mark 10:45, where the Son of man, a royal figure in the Gospels, comes not to be served but to serve (likely an ironic reversal of Dan. 7:13-14, where peoples "serve" the "one like a son of man"). The same sacrificial spirit animates the stories of Jesus approaching the city of Jerusalem. When the Son of David makes his royal entrance, he rides humbly on a donkey instead of a war horse. He has not in any conventional sense overpowered anybody or anything, nor is he about to do so. Like the God he represents, he is not that sort of ruler. This is no conquering king but the author of the beatitudes. We un-derstand why Matthew has Jesus decline the assistance of militant an-gels and declare that those who take the sword will perish by the sword (Matt. 26:52-53). The politics of heaven are not the politics of earth.

In line with all this is Matt. 17:24-27, where Jesus, in discussing the

---

2. On this matter I have learned from Richard Bauckham, "Kingdom and Church ac-cording to Jesus and Paul," *Horizons in Biblical Theology* 18 (1996): 1-27.

temple tax, asks, "From whom do kings of the earth take toll or tribute? From their children or from others?" Although the paragraph assumes that God is a king, Peter's answer — "from others" — and Jesus' response — "then the sons are free" — indicate that God relates to the disciples not as a potentate to exploited subjects but as a father to privileged members of his family.

So although a king, God is even more a father, and a father in that he is profoundly kind and merciful. This is in fact the heart and soul of Jesus' theology. When the rain falls, this is a sign that the merciful Father in heaven is good to everyone, the unjust as well as the just (Matt. 5:43-48). When Jesus promises that those who seek will find, this is due to his conviction that the Father in heaven gives good gifts to his children (Matt. 7:7-11 = Luke 11:9-13). When the prodigal son returns not to censure but to celebration, this is because his father, a cipher for God, loves in a way that defeats all other considerations (Luke 15:11-32).

From whence did Jesus derive his deep-seated conviction that God is like a benevolent father and so above all loving and unexpectedly gracious? Although we can say next to nothing about his upbringing, one might speculate that, without memories of a happy relationship with his earthly father, Jesus would not have insistently depicted the divinity as a kind father.

Beyond this, we do know that Jesus inherited the idea of God as a compassionate father from his Jewish tradition. Ps. 103:13 speaks of God as "a father who has compassion on his children." The Thanksgiving Hymns from the Dead Sea Scrolls contain this touching confession: "For you are a father to all [the sons] of your truth, and as a woman who tenderly loves her baby, so do you rejoice in them; and as a foster-father bears a child in his lap, so do you care for all of your creatures" (1QH 17[9].35-36). The targum on Isa. 63:16 declares that God's mercies are "greater than those of a father toward his sons."

Perhaps his theological tradition, which resonated with his youthful experience at home, suffices to account for Jesus' stress upon God as a loving Father. Yet one can hardly refrain from conjecturing that something more may have been involved. It is well known that people sometimes find themselves in an altered state of consciousness in which they feel the overwhelming presence of an intense, all-encompassing love. The experience is cross-cultural and common enough. It is scarcely confined to the reveries of mystics and saints such as Mansur al-Hallaj, Richard

Rolle, and Teresa of Avila. One sociologist in the 1970s found that, of North Americans who reported having one or more "mystical" experiences, fully forty-three percent said that it brought "the conviction that love is at the center of everything."[3] Here is one modern person's account: "The kitchen and the garden were filled with golden light. I became conscious that at the center of the Universe, and in my garden, was a great pulsing dynamo that ceaselessly poured out love. This love poured over and through me, and I was part of it and it wholly encompassed me."[4]

These words recount something more than a peaceful moment when nature seems "to wrap us round with friendliness" (William James), the sort of moment we can almost induce by going to the right place at the right time. They rather witness to something over which we have no control, something that comes out of the blue, an inexplicable intrusion from some tenderly affectionate, seemingly transcendent Reality. This is how another described the experience:

> One day, I was sweeping the stairs, down in the house in which I was working, when suddenly I was overcome, overwhelmed, saturated . . . with a sense of the most sublime and living love. It not only affected me, but seemed to bring everything around me to life. The brush in my hand, my dustpan, the stairs, seemed to come alive with love. I seemed no longer me, with my petty troubles and trials, but part of this infinite power of love, so utterly overwhelming and wonderful that one knew at once what the saints had grasped.[5]

Having been unaccountably favored with this same sort of rapture myself on a couple of occasions, I know that, whatever the explanation, it is subjectively real, overpoweringly so.

3. Andrew M. Greeley, *The Sociology of the Paranormal: A Reconnaissance* (Beverly Hills, CA/London: Sage, 1975), p. 65.

4. Meg Maxwell and Verena Tschudin, eds., *Seeing the Invisible: Modern Religious and Other Transcendent Experiences* (London: Arkana, 1990), p. 56. The writer continues: "The vision was gone in a moment, leaving me with a strong desire to rush out and embrace anyone I could find. . . . It was overwhelmingly real, more real than anything I had experienced. . . . The vision was of a far 'realler' quality. To deny it would be the ultimate sin, blasphemy." For similar experiences see pp. 18, 25, 55, 61-63, 137.

5. David Hay, *Something There: The Biology of the Human Spirit* (Philadelphia: Templeton Foundation Press, 2007), pp. 18-19.

Whether or not Jesus had numinous experiences that confirmed him in his understanding of God as intense, universal compassion — a proposition we can only entertain, not argue for or against — he more than made his own the traditional notion that God's chief attribute is an all-inclusive loving-kindness.

Those of us so inclined may find solace in this theology. Others, however, will view it as nearly absurd, because it comes up so hard against the innumerable woes of real life. Every blessing is balanced by some curse. The one-time appeal of Manichaeism, with its enduring clash between a good God and a bad God, requires no explanation. What needs accounting for is why cosmic dualism has gone out of fashion: it makes such good sense. Likewise sensible is denial of any deity, at least a good deity.

Jesus' sort of God has, understandably enough, taken a beating in recent centuries. Pierre Bayle, writing that human beings are "wicked and miserable," that "prisons, hospitals, gallows, and beggars" are everywhere, and that "history is nothing but the crimes and misfortunes of mankind," confessed inability to harmonize the world's agony with God's goodness;[6] and Leibnitz's rejoinder on God's behalf, that this is the best of all possible worlds, was readily mocked by Voltaire. Feuerbach and Freud thought it evident that the image of a loving Father in heaven stems from self-deception: it is a projection created by our yearning for parental protection in what is in truth an unfeeling, unsympathetic universe. Rabbi Richard Rubenstein argued that, because the God of Israel, who heard the cry of the slaves in Egypt and delivered them from bondage, did not hear the cry of the Jews in Germany and deliver them from the ovens, no such God exists. Rubenstein gave up the God of history for the silence of mysticism. And the contemporary philosopher William Rowe has reformulated the argument from evil in this form, which has been so much discussed because its force is so patent:

1. There exist instances of intense suffering which an omnipotent, omniscient being could have prevented without thereby losing some greater good or permitting some evil equally bad or worse.

6. Pierre Bayle, "Manicheans; Note D," in *The Problem of Evil: A Reader*, ed. Mark Larrimore (Malden, MA/Oxford, UK/Victoria, Australia: Blackwell, 2002), p. 186.

2. An omniscient, wholly good being would prevent the occurrence of any intense suffering it could, unless it could not do so without thereby losing some greater good or permitting some evil equally bad or worse.

3. There does not exist an omnipotent, omniscient, wholly good being.[7]

However one responds to the arguments of Rowe, Rubenstein, Freud, Feuerbach, and Bayle, Jesus' assertion of God's goodness is not, to say the least, transparently obvious. This is partly why many Christians would say that their faith in his God is just that, faith.

Now it would be inane to expect a first-century Jew to have pre-packaged, for our later use, apt answers to modern formulations of the problem of evil. Jesus was not a philosopher, nor did he precognitively address directly the issues of a later time and place. This does not mean, however, that he has nothing at all to say to us on the vexed subject at hand. In fact, the memories about him offer, I suggest, some wisdom in the matter of what is perhaps the most intractable problem for Christian faith.

To begin with, Jesus was not Candide. His eyes were wide open. He saw and felt the omnipresent pain and evil around him, and the sources nowhere have him optimistically insisting that "Health is more common than sickness: Pleasure than pain: Happiness than misery," or that "for one vexation which we meet with, we attain, upon computation, a hundred enjoyments."[8] Jesus rather promoted his God of grace and mercy in the midst of a trying world, one in which, as his words observe, the poor are always with us, in which children are set against parents and parents against children, in which Pilate ruthlessly executes Galileans and a building collapses upon Jerusalemites (Mark 14:7; Matt. 10:34-36 = Luke 12:51-53; Luke 13:1-5). Jesus was under no illusion that things were going well or that obedience to God would fill us with sweetness and light. He may have instructed his followers to pray "Deliver us from evil," but he foresaw for himself and others hardship and persecution. "If they have

7. William L. Rowe, "The Problem of Evil and Some Varieties of Atheism," *American Philosophical Quarterly* 16 (1979): 336.

8. So Cleanthes, the defender of God, in David Hume, *Dialogues Concerning Natural Religion,* ed. Norman Kemp Smith (Indianapolis, IN: Bobbs-Merrill, 1947), p. 200.

called the master of the house Beelzebul, how much more will they ma-
lign those of his household" (Matt. 10:25). He may have told people to
turn the other cheek, but he did not assure them that this would convert
enemies into friends. "Expect nothing in return" (Luke 6:35). He may
have taught that God cares for the sparrow, but he knew that the sparrow nonetheless falls to the ground. "Brother will betray brother to
death" (Mark 13:12). That Jesus was not naive, that he was keenly alive to
the pain and troubles of the world, seems confirmed by the sayings in
which he speaks of Satan and the stories in which he casts out evil spir-
its. Jesus knew a world with devils filled.

Not only did Jesus prudently not discount the ills around him, but
the tradition nowhere has him accounting for or justifying evil. That is,
none of his words construct a theodicy. He surely assumed that demons
explain demoniacs, but to our knowledge he left demons unexplained.
Maybe he believed them to be fallen angels. Or maybe he believed them
to be the offspring of the mating of the sons of God with the daughters of
men (Gen. 6:1-4). Or maybe he thought something else, or maybe nothing at all about the subject.

The point for us is that the tradition about him has no interest in
explaining or rationalizing evil. Indeed, Luke 13:1-5 has Jesus ask, "Do
you think that because these Galileans suffered in this way they were
worse sinners than all other Galileans?" Tragedy is not picky; it just happens. Similarly, John 9:1-12 remembers Jesus as refusing to make calam-
ity the upshot of sin. "Who sinned, this man or his parents, that he was
born blind?" the disciples ask Jesus. His answer negates their two pro-
posals: "Neither this man nor his parents sinned." Perhaps Jesus intu-
ited, like the authors of Job and 4 Ezra, that misfortune blows where it
wills, that it defies rational explanation, that we can no more fathom it
than we can count the number of hairs on our heads (Matt. 10:30 = Luke
12:7).[9] However that may be, Jesus did not, to our knowledge, commit
himself to any rationalization that might pretend to downplay evil or
draw its sting.

This should come as no surprise, because the tradition, as before related, is overflowing with eschatological expectation. Such expectation
implicitly concedes that life as we have known it does not make sense. It

9. For this interpretation of Matt. 10:30 = Luke 12:7 see Dale C. Allison, Jr., *The Jesus
Tradition in Q* (Harrisburg, PA: Trinity Press Intl., 1997), pp. 168-75.

posits reward and punishment in a life to come precisely because they are missing from the here and now. It locates meaning in the future because there is a deficiency of sense in the present. It hopes for better someday because today it is worse.

Eschatology does nothing, of course, to explain away evil, and it leaves us with the question, Why should God be better to all in the future than God seems to be now? To which Jesus prudently returns no answer. But he does share with us his audacious imagination, born of his unswerving conviction that, despite appearances, God is profoundly good. His fundamental intuition is that the creator must be the redeemer, that the divine Father is good enough to ensure that those who mourn will be comforted, loving enough to guarantee that those who weep now will someday laugh. The world cannot be a fait accompli; it must instead be an impermanent stage on the way to some time and place in which God will be all in all. Jesus is relentlessly optimistic about "eternal life" because he is relentlessly optimistic about his God, who "is God not of the dead, but of the living" (Mark 12:27).

We do well, I suggest, to follow his lead. For although eschatology is not the solution to the problem of evil, without eschatology there can be no solution. If what we see on this earth is all that we will ever see, if there is no further repairing of wrongs beyond what we have already witnessed, then divine love and justice do not really count for much.

This is not, for me, a theological cliché but a philosophical necessity. If the sufferings of the present time are never eclipsed, if there is nothing beyond tragedy and the monotony of death, then I for one do not believe that Jesus' good God exists. But as I do believe in his God, I must believe in a resurrection of the dead or, if I may echo Plato, something like it. In the words of Rabbi Cohn-Sherbok, we require eschatology if we are

> to make sense of the world as the creation of an all-good and all-powerful God. Without the eventual vindication of the righteous in Paradise, there is no way to sustain belief in a providential God who watches over His chosen people. The essence of the Jewish understanding of God is that He loves His chosen people. If death means extinction, there is no way to make sense of the claim that He loves and cherishes all those who died in the concentration camps — suffering and death would ultimately triumph on each of those who perished. But if there is eternal life

in a World to Come, then there is hope that the righteous will share in a divine life.[10]

I have no idea what the realization of God's dream, which Jesus called the kingdom of God, will look like. For that we have only intimations and religious myths. And I am fully aware (as Jesus was not) of the many scientific and philosophical issues raised by belief in a world beyond or after this one. But hope for something more than death's wanton and cruel negation of life seems necessary if Jesus' belief in God's loving-kindness is to ring true. Such hope is also, I have come to believe, a correlate of Jesus' demand that I love my neighbor and live by the golden rule. For to love others and to desire for them what I desire for myself is to wish them well, and if they are well, I can hardly want them to go out of existence.

One final comment on Jesus and his eschatological response to evil. Many people, including some Christians, have, especially since Nietzsche, objected that eschatological hope is escapist, that it impoverishes the present and discourages ardent efforts to ameliorate human ills. One sees the point. Much that has gone under the name of Christianity sadly gives substance to the reproach. As one nineteenth-century writer observed of his experience:

> Those who stick closest to the Scripture do not shrink from saying, that "it is not worth while trying to mend the world," and stigmatize as "political and worldly" such as pursue an opposite course. Undoubtedly, if we are to expect our Master at cockcrowing, we shall not study the permanent improvement of this transitory scene. To teach the certain speedy destruction of earthly things, as the New Testament does, is to cut the sinews of all earthly progress; to declare war against Intellect and Imagination, [and] against . . . Social advancement.[11]

But this protest does not sound right if transferred from some of Jesus' followers to Jesus himself. For his faith in the world to come did not

---

10. Dan Cohn-Sherbok, "Jewish Faith and the Holocaust," *Religious Studies* 26 (1990): 292.

11. Francis Newman, *Phases of Faith* (New York: Humanities Press, 1970; reprint of 1850 edition), p. 136 (italics deleted).

take him out of the world but rather, from what we can tell, all the further into it. He did not proclaim the wonderful things to come and then pass by on the other side of the road. He rather turned his eschatological ideal into an ethical blueprint for compassionate ministry in the present, which means that, in addition to saying that things would get better, he set about making it so. "Go and tell John what you have seen and heard: the blind receive their sight, the lame walk, the lepers are cleansed, the deaf hear, the dead are raised, the poor have good news brought to them" (Luke 7:22). Although Jesus failed to explain evil, he did not fail to fight it. Matthew's version of the Lord's Prayer gets it right: whoever prays "your kingdom come" must also see to it that "your will be done, on earth as it is in heaven" (6:10).

Jesus' eschatological hope and his humanitarianism cannot be sundered because they were both products of his infatuation with divine love. God's loving devotion to the world requires that it not suffer disrepair forever, and God's love shed abroad in human hearts, a love that fosters self-transcendence, cannot wait for heaven to come to earth: it must, before the end, feed the hungry and clothe the naked.

Imagination: Ought over Is

For Jesus, meaning resides principally in the heavenly Father and in the world to come, and in their light he perceives and understands everything else. He views earth from the vantage point of heaven, and he interprets the present by projecting himself into the future and then looking back. The world's chief values are not intrinsic but extrinsic; they reside in the God who is above the world and within the world and waiting at its end.

Because his God is in heaven and because the world to come has not yet come, neither reality is visible. So Jesus, like Paul in 2 Cor. 4:18, looks not to the things seen but to the things unseen. It is understandable that Jesus is above all an author of parables and a devotee of the imagination: he cannot report but only imagine. It is also understandable that he sallies forth against the ordinary.

Everyday life is ruled by custom, habit, and routine, and these all too readily cultivate a God-obscuring stasis. Unless one realizes that things are not what they seem to be and that they will not be as they are forever, one will miss what matters most and substitute a god of lesser value and meaning. The rich man, anxious for control and security, said, "Soul, you have ample goods laid up for many years; relax, eat, drink, be merry." But God said to him: "You fool! This very night your life is being demanded of you. And the things you have prepared, whose will they be?" (Luke 12:19-20). People can gain the whole superficial world and yet lose their own souls.

Because he believes that one cannot serve God and mammon, or God and anything else for that matter (Matt. 6:24; Luke 16:13), the God-intoxicated Jesus incessantly proclaims the one thing needful. His parables and aphorisms reveal that the heavenly trumps the earthly and that the future will trump the present, and that we are encompassed by empty and dangerous distractions. "Do not store up for yourselves treasures on earth, where moth and rust consume and where thieves break in and steal; but store up for yourselves treasures in heaven, where neither moth nor rust consumes and where thieves do not break in and steal. For where your treasure is, there your heart will be also" (Matt. 6:19-21). Jesus urges his hearers to cast aside all but the relentless, single-minded pursuit of what should be their ultimate concern. "The kingdom of heaven is like a merchant in search of fine pearls; on finding one pearl of great value, he went and sold all that he had and bought it" (Matt. 13:45-46).

Jesus proclaims the new because the old is not enough (Mark 2:21-22). He turns the world over because he thinks that it is upside down (Matt. 20:16; Mark 10:31; Luke 13:30). He disorients that he might reorient. This requires confronting the ordinary with the extraordinary, at which he is an expert.

The tradition has him doing any number of peculiar things. He shares meals with people who might well be shunned, including, according to his critics, robbers for the state (Matt. 11:19; Mark 2:16; Luke 7:34). He calls Peter and others to forsake their livelihoods, indeed to break off work in the middle of their labors to follow him (Matt. 8:18-21; Mark 1:16-20; 2:13-14; Luke 9:57-62). He heals people on the Sabbath, no doubt intending to provoke debate and opposition, at which he succeeds (Mark 2:23-28; 3:1-6; Luke 14:1-6). He turns tables over in the temple, declaring no more business as usual (Mark 11:15-19; John 2:13-17).

His speech is equally suffused by oddities. There are his startling imperatives — "Leave the dead to bury their own dead" (Matt. 8:22; Luke

9:60); "Hate your father and your mother" (Luke 14:26); "Love your enemies" (Matt. 5:44; Luke 6:27); "Greet no one on the road" (Luke 10:4).
There are his unexpected generalizations — "Blessed are those who
mourn" (Matt. 5:4); "The last will be first" (Matt. 20:16; Mark 10:31; Luke
13:30); "I have come not to bring peace but a sword" (Matt. 10:34; Luke
12:51); "There are eunuchs who have made themselves eunuchs for the
sake of the kingdom of heaven" (Matt. 19:12). And there are the memorable stories with unanticipated turns. We read of the Samaritan who, unlike his pious Jewish counterparts, displays charity (Luke 10:29-37); of the
irrational employer who pays all laborers the same wage, regardless of
hours worked (Matt. 20:1-16); of the dishonest manager who earns praise
for his flagrantly sinful actions (Luke 16:1-13); and of the long-suffering father who welcomes home the prodigal without a word of reprimand
(Luke 15:11-32). "Jesus," in Funk's words, "detypifies" and "defamiliarizes"
common perceptions. He says the unexpected. He confounds by contra-
dicting what everybody already knows, by reversing those common-
places his audience has just endorsed with their assent to his opening
lines."[12]

Persuaded that the true nature of things is not obvious, Jesus, in
word and deed, sets out with gusto to fracture the hypnotic hold of life-
as-it-has-always-been. He endeavors, in Coleridge's words, to awaken
our minds "from the lethargy of custom" and to remove "the film of fa-
miliarity and selfish solicitude that covers our eyes."[13] He seeks to shift
attention, to alter perception, to expand awareness, to change behavior.
"Repent, for the kingdom of heaven is at hand" (Matt. 4:17). This is a call
to abandon rote behavior, to forsake reflexive ways.

Because he sanctions not the world as it is but only the world as it
should be, he dislikes the default setting of ordinary consciousness,
whose defect is precisely that it accepts the present world as the real
world. He is disconcerted that people see without seeing (Mark 4:12; 8:18)
and that so few strive to enter through the narrow gate (Matt. 7:13-14;
Luke 13:23-24). He mourns that his hearers, wedded to everyday life and
worrying so little about God's reign, fret so much about food and cloth-

12. Robert W. Funk, *Honest to Jesus: Jesus for a New Millennium* (San Francisco:
HarperSanFrancisco, 1996), p. 154.
13. Samuel Taylor Coleridge, *Biographia Literaria*, in The Collected Works of Samuel
Taylor Coleridge 7; Bollingen Series 75; ed. James Engell and W. Jackson Bate (Princeton:
Princeton University Press, 1983), 2:6-7.

ing (Matt. 6:25-34; Luke 12:22-31). He grieves that they find so much comfort in material trinkets and set their hope on a world that is passing away, thereby running the risk of missing the life that is really life.

All of this makes Jesus, from one point of view, otherworldly, a trait many no longer reckon a virtue. Yet we must remember that he does not retire to the wilderness, nor does he set up a community on the shores of the Dead Sea. He may be an itinerant with nowhere to lay his head, but he does not forsake the world at large. He and his fellow missionaries go from village to village, not from deserted place to deserted place. And he calls only some who believe in him to abandon work and kin to follow him literally. The rest need only follow his counsel. They are to live their new lives where they have lived their old ones. Like Zacchaeus, they do not exit their worlds but redeem them, bringing into their communities Jesus' vision of the divine future, which in his speech becomes God's demand for benevolence and justice right now (Luke 19:1-10).

Synthesis: The Coincidence of Opposites

The basic sequence of Jewish eschatology appears again and again in the sayings attributed to Jesus: suffering then vindication, tribulation then blessedness, death then life:

- "Blessed are you who are hungry now, for you will be filled" (Luke 6:21; *Gospel of Thomas* 69).
- "Blessed are those who mourn, for they will be comforted" (Matt. 5:4; Luke 6:21).
- "Blessed are you when people revile you and persecute you and utter all kinds of evil against you falsely on my account. Rejoice and be glad, for your reward is great in heaven" (Matt. 5:11-12; Luke 6:22-23).
- "Those who humble themselves will be exalted" (Matt. 18:4; 23:12; Luke 14:11; 18:14).
- "Those who lose their life will keep it" (Matt. 10:39; Mark 8:35; Luke 17:33).
- "The last will be first" (Mark 10:31; *Gospel of Thomas* 4).
- "The Son of man is to be betrayed into human hands, and they will kill him, and three days after being killed, he will rise again" (Mark 9:31).

- "But in those days, after that suffering . . . they will see the Son of man coming in clouds with great power and glory" (Mark 13:24-26).

Part of the reason that Jesus so fascinates and inspires is that his life incarnates the eschatological pattern. He is the coincidence of opposites, embodying in his own person the extremes of apocalyptic expectation, which means the extremes of human experience. He is the first who becomes last and the last who becomes first.

On the one hand, Jesus announces and makes real the eschatological presence of the God of Israel. Satan has fallen like lightning from heaven and the demons are being routed (Matt. 12:25-29; Mark 1:21-28; 3:23-30; 5:1-20; Luke 10:18; 11:17-22). The lame walk and the blind see (Matt. 11:5; Mark 2:1-12; 10:46-52; Luke 7:22). Lepers are cleansed and those in poverty are cheered with good news (Matt. 11:5; Mark 1:40-45; Luke 7:22). The long-awaited kingdom of God has arrived and there is no time to fast, only to make merry: the bridegroom is here (Matt. 12:28; Mark 2:18-19; Luke 11:20; 17:20). Expectant crowds naturally follow Jesus everywhere (Mark 1:32-34; 2:1, 13; 3:7; 5:21; John 12:9), and elation, gratitude, and amazement seize them by turns (Matt. 11:25; Mark 2:12; 4:41; 5:20, 42; Luke 10:17, 21; 17:16). Even death does not put an end to all the celebration, for death is swallowed up in victory, and there is reunion with forgiven friends (Matt. 28:1-20; Mark 16:1-8; Luke 24:1-53; John 20-21). The old world is ashes; the new world has come.

On the other hand, that is only half of the story. Paradoxically, the joyful Jesus is familiar with sorrows and acquainted with grief. He has nowhere to lay his head (Matt. 8:20; Luke 9:58). People abuse him with insults (Matt. 11:19; Mark 2:16; 3:30; Luke 7:34). Respected leaders assail his teachings and behavior (Mark 2:1-12, 23-28). Others turn a deaf ear to his appeals (Matt. 11:20-24; Mark 6:1-6; Luke 10:13-15). John the Baptist, a man he hails as more than a prophet, is arrested, imprisoned, and beheaded (Mark 6:17-29). Ever since then, the kingdom of God suffers violence (Matt. 11:12). His own companions misunderstand (Mark 7:18; 8:14-21, 31-33; 9:32; 10:13-16). Eventually, one of them — "one of the twelve," as Mark says several times — betrays him to his enemies (Mark 14:1-2, 17-21, 43-53). The others, in his hour of desperation, confusedly run away, leaving him alone — except for Peter, who spinelessly follows from a distance and then denies ever knowing him (Mark 14:66-72; John 18:15-18, 25-27). Pagan soldiers whip Jesus, mock him, and nail him to an instrument of torture (Mark 15:15, 24). Unfeeling crowds file by and stare, hurling ridicule (Mark 15:29-31). Finally, he dies un-Socratically, seemingly disillusioned, feeling as though God — the good Father who is kind to all, the good Father who opens the door to those who knock, the good Father who takes care of the lilies and the ravens and should all the more take care of the saints (Luke 6:35; Matt. 7:7-11 = Luke 11:9-13; Matt. 6:25-34 = Luke 12:22-31) — has forsaken him (Mark 15:34). His end is physical torment and mental anguish, loss of life and loss of meaning.

So the tradition gives us a Jesus who knows how to laugh loudly and to wail miserably, a Jesus who knows the presence of God and the absence of God, a Jesus who experiences what some of us find long before we die: both heaven and hell.

That Jesus is big enough to take in the extremes of human experience makes him both sympathetic and convincing. Any credible interpretation of human existence must come to terms with the acute polarities that characterize most of our lives. Even in the midst of our relative prosperity, anxiety and anger by turns grip us; malevolence and foolishness greet us daily; sin and guilt never leave us. Physical pain and mental pain haunt our lives, and we are ever the victims of the senseless sport of circumstance: something is always going wrong, when not for us then for others we love. And over it all is spread the eternal shroud of death. We blossom and flourish and wither and perish. Our cruel fate is to close our eyes and become short-term memories.

And yet, in the midst of such universal misfortune and heartbreak, an inscrutable Providence allows us sometimes to behold the good, the true, and the beautiful, enables us to happen upon friendship and love, laughter and delight, knowledge and wisdom; and those of us with religious faith may further believe that, through some enigmatic grace, we have sometimes encountered the ineffable presence of a loving God. So human experience in general and religious experience in particular offer intense paradoxes. Maybe this is what Pascal was getting at when he wrote, "It is incomprehensible that God exists, and it is incomprehensible that he does not exist."[14]

Jesus' words and life give fitting expression to all this. The extremes of human experience are such that they are effectively represented by the

---

14. Blaise Pascal, *Pensées,* Introduction and notes by Ch.-Marc des Granges (Paris: Gernier Frères, 1964), p. 134.

extremes of eschatological expectation and by a life of celebration and crucifixion. If Jesus had pretended to know only the blessings of the future age, we should turn our backs on him, for we would know his faith to be a hopeless flight from the pain and dread of living. And if he had harped only on death's doom and the tribulation of the latter days, we would have to judge his hope too small, the distance between him and God too great. But it was otherwise. By announcing not only tribulation present and coming but also salvation present and coming and then by living into both, Jesus commends himself to us.

One last thought. Although Jesus may be the coincidence of opposites, he does not reconcile or unify them. For him, death and life are not like summer and winter, the one always coming after the other, in an eternal return, without victor. He may believe in the devil, but he believes far more in God. Jesus' dualism is relative, not absolute. There can be no tie, for evil is bound to lose. The divine love and goodness must triumph over all else. So the opposites are not complementary but antagonistic, not equal but sequential: in the end, the good undoes the bad. And in this, as in so much else, Jesus' life instantiates his teaching. For the resurrection does not balance crucifixion and the grave. It defeats them.

Index of Modern Names

Abrams, M. H., 33
Adams, Edward, 99n.15
Allison, Dale C., Jr., 16-17, 64n.6, 99n.15, 110n.9
Alvarado, Carlos S., 74n.11

Barth, Karl, 7-8, 12
Bate, W. Jackson, 115n.13
Bauckham, Richard, 105n.2
Bayle, Pierre, 108-9
Benedict XVI, 86
Bengel, Albrecht, 84
Blomberg, Craig, 58
Borg, Marcus, 8, 12, 46, 87-88
Bultmann, Rudolf, 12, 37, 69, 91
Bundy, Walter, 87

Calvin, John, 2, 84
Chamberlin, T. C., 58
Chesterton, G. K., 11, 53
Cohn-Sherbok, Dan, 111-12
Coleridge, Samuel Taylor, 115
Crossan, John Dominic, 7-8, 11, 19, 26, 28, 35-36, 59, 91
Cullmann, Oscar, 13, 31n.1, 91

Dodd, C. H., 10, 59, 91

Engell, James, 115n.13

Feuerbach, Ludwig, 108-9
Freud, Sigmund, 108-9
Funk, Robert, 6-7, 17-21, 64, 88-89, 115

Gale, Richard, 1
Golitzin, Alexander, 74n.11
Granges, Ch.-Marc des, 118n.14
Greeley, Andrew M., 107n.3

Hanson, K. C., 7n.3
Hanson, R. P. C., 85n.4
Haraldsson, Erlendur, 73n.9
Harnack, Adolf, 15
Hay, David, 1, 107n.5
Hengel, Martin, 88
Hick, John, 87n.6
Hill, H. Erskine, 96-97
Hume, David, 68, 109n.8

James, William, 79, 107
Jeremias, Joachim, 7, 27, 59, 91

Keats, John, 32-33
Knox, John, 87
Kuhlman, Kathryn, 76
Kümmel, Werner, 91

Lewis, C. S., 36

Liebnitz, Gottfried Wilhelm Freiherr
  von, 108
Lincoln, Abraham, 24, 47
Loofs, Friedrich, 53
Luria, Alexander, 23
Luther, Martin, 2, 47, 97

Manson, T. W., 10
Maxwell, Meg, 107n.4
Meier, John, 15
Motovilov, Nicholas, 72-74

Nagel, Thomas, 31
Neimar, Susan, 104
Newman, Carey C., 99n.15
Newman, Francis, 112n.11
Nietzsche, Friedrich, 112

Pannenberg, Wolfhart, 12
Pascal, Blaise, 118
Paulus, Heinrich Eberhard Gottlob, 3
Pio, Padre, 76
Pius X, 96

Reimarus, Hermann Samuel, 3, 7, 69, 90
Roberts, Oral, 76
Robinson, Marilynne, 6
Rowe, William, 108-9
Rubenstein, Richard, 108-9

Sanders, E. P., 8, 11, 60
Saranam, Sankara, 36, 37n.10
Schacter, Daniel L., 62n.5
Schweitzer, Albert, 3, 7-8, 12, 15, 27, 48,
  59, 87, 89, 91-92, 95-97
Seraphim of Sarov, 72-73
Smith, Joseph, 37
Smith, Norman Kemp, 109n.8
Smith, Wilfred Cantwell, 31
Sri Baba, 73
Stanford, W. B., 33
Strauss, David Friedrich, 3, 7, 69, 76,
  86, 90
Streeter, B. H., 98-99

Taylor, Vincent, 10
Tillich, Paul, 7-8, 12
Thurston, Herbert, 74n.10
Treece, Patricia, 74n.11
Tschudin, Verena, 107n.4

Victoria, Queen, 47

Weaver, Walter P., 3n.5
Weiss, Johannes, 3, 90-92, 97
Wigner, Eugene, 6
Wright, G. Ernest, 31n.1
Wright, N. T. (Tom), 8, 11, 20-22, 46,
  88n.9, 91
Zander, Valentine, 73n.8

Index of Scripture

OLD TESTAMENT

Genesis

1	39
5:18	28
5:21-24	28
6:1-4	110

Exodus

8:19	65
24:1	69
24:9-11	69
24:15-18	69
24:16	69
34:5	69
34:29-30	69
34:30	69
34:35	69

Numbers

23:19	81

Deuteronomy

18:15	69
18:18	69

2 Samuel

12:3	34

Job

1:1	34
9:8	90

Psalms

22	26
65:7	80
69	26
77:19	80
89:9	80
103:13	106
110:1	64

Proverbs

19:17	51

Isaiah

7:14	36
26:19	78, 95
29:18-19	78, 95
35:5-6	78, 95
42:18	78, 95
61	65, 95
61:1	95
61:1-2	78
63:16	106

Ezekiel

18:20	35

Daniel

7	64, 94
7:13	64
7:13-14	105

Zechariah

9:9	36
13:7	95

Malachi

3:1	95
4:5-6	95

NEW TESTAMENT

Matthew

3:11-12	90, 95
3:15	56
4	25
4:1-11	25, 67, 84
4:5-11	2n.2
4:17	115
4:23-25	68
5-7	2
5:3	95
5:4	95, 115-16
5:6	95
5:8	47

5:11-12	95, 116	10:32-33	64, 90, 94	18:6-7	92
5:12	93	10:34	115	18:8-9	92
5:17	95	10:34-36	94, 109	18:20	51
5:19	93	10:37	63	18:21-22	63
5:20	93	10:38	63	19:11-12	63
5:21-26	28	10:39	63, 93, 116	19:12	115
5:22	92	10:40	65	19:19	28
5:33-37	63	11:2-4	65	19:28	64-65, 94
5:38-42	28	11:2-5	67, 78, 90, 95	20:1-16	115
5:38-48	62, 102	11:4-6	12	20:16	114-15
5:42	63	11:5	117	20:23	84
5:43-48	28, 106	11:10	94	21:21	28
5:44	115	11:12	117	22:7	56
6:10	93, 113	11:12-13	94	22:13	92
6:19-21	114	11:19	114, 117	22:34-40	28
6:22-23	28	11:20-24	117	23:10	94
6:24	114	11:21	67	23:12	93, 116
6:25-34	116, 118	11:21-24	65	23:13	93
7:1-2	62	11:22	92	23:15	92
7:6	57	11:24	92	23:33	92
7:7-11	106, 118	11:25	117	23:34-35	92
7:13	94	11:27	80	24-25	100
7:13-14	115	11:29	48	24:36	82-83, 96
7:19	92	12:22-42	67	24:37-39	92
7:21	93	12:25-29	117	24:40-41	92
7:21-27	65	12:27-28	67	24:43-51	94
8:5-13	67	12:28	65, 93, 117	24:45-51	92
8:11-12	94	12:33-35	28	24:51	92
8:18-21	114	12:36	92	25	51
8:20	117	12:41-42	94	25:1-13	94
8:21-22	62	13	23	25:29	93
8:22	114	13:12	93	25:30	92
9:27-31	67	13:24-30	93	25:31-46	50-51, 56, 93
9:32-34	67	13:36-43	93	26:52-53	105
10	2	13:41	92	27:46	85
10:7	93	13:45-46	114	27:51-53	21, 72
10:8	67	13:47-50	93	28:1-20	117
10:9-10	62	14:22-33	44	28:11-15	3
10:10	62	14:28-33	72	28:20	51
10:15	65, 92	15:7-20	28		
10:23	64, 92, 100	16:19	84	**Mark**	
10:25	110	17:20	28, 67	1:12-13	80, 84
10:28	92	17:24-27	67, 105	1:15	93
10:30	110	18:4	116	1:16-20	63, 114

1:21-28	117	7:18	117	10:39-40	84
1:21-38	67	7:24-30	67	10:42-43	105
1:29-31	67	7:31-37	67	10:45	105
1:32-34	117	8:1-10	67	10:46-52	67, 117
1:40-45	67, 117	8:14-21	117	11:9-10	64, 94
2:1	117	8:18	115	11:12-14	67
2:1-12	67, 117	8:22-26	67	11:15-19	114
2:12	117	8:23	80	11:20-24	67
2:13	117	8:27-29	46	11:22-23	67
2:13-14	114	8:27-30	94	11:23	28
2:14	63	8:29	64	12:1-12	56
2:16	114, 117	8:31-33	117	12:18-27	94
2:18-19	117	8:34	63	12:27	111
2:21-22	114	8:35	63, 93, 116	12:28-34	51
2:23-28	114, 117	8:38	64	13	2, 27, 100
3:1-6	67, 114	9:1	92, 100	13:2	27
3:5	80	9:2	69	13:3-23	94
3:7	117	9:2-3	69	13:9	27
3:7-12	68	9:2-8	67	13:12	110
3:13-19	64	9:5	69, 75	13:24	27
3:15	67	9:7	69, 78	13:24-26	117
3:23-30	117	9:13	95	13:26	38-39, 94
3:30	117	9:14-29	67	13:26-27	64
4:12	115	9:16	80	13:27	92
4:25	93	9:21	80	13:30	92, 100
4:35-41	67, 80	9:31	116	13:32	80, 82-83, 96
4:38	80	9:32	117	13:33-37	94
4:41	117	9:33	80	13:35-36	27
5:1-20	67, 117	9:42	92	14	27
5:9	80	9:42-48	63	14:1-2	117
5:20	117	9:43-45	92	14:7	109
5:21	117	9:43-47	93	14:17-21	117
5:21-24	67	9:47-48	92	14:25	94
5:25-34	67	9:49	92	14:27	95
5:30	80	10:2-9	62	14:32-42	80
5:35-43	67	10:13-16	117	14:34-42	27
5:42	117	10:15	93	14:41	27
6:1-6	117	10:17-27	63	14:43-53	117
6:8-9	62	10:23	93	14:53-65	27
6:17-29	117	10:23-25	93	14:58	64
6:30-44	67	10:29-30	93	14:61-62	64
6:38	80	10:30	94	14:62	64, 90, 94
6:45-51	67	10:31	93, 114-16	14:65	27
6:45-52	80	10:35-40	64	14:66-72	117

15   26-27

15:1-15   27

15:2   65, 94

15:6   26

15:9   94

15:15   118

15:18   94

15:24   118

15:26   94

15:29-31   118

15:32   94

15:33   27

15:34   80, 85, 118

15:38   27

16:1-8   117

Luke

2:52   80, 84

3:16-17   90

4   25

4:1-13   25, 67, 84

4:5-13   2n.2

4:16-19   65, 95

5:1-11   67

5:15   68

6:20-23   95

6:21   116

6:22-23   116

6:23   93

6:24   57

6:27   115

6:27-36   62

6:35   110, 118

6:37-38   62

6:46-49   65

7:1-10   67

7:11-17   67

7:16-17   95

7:18-23   65, 67, 78, 90, 95

7:22   113, 117

7:22-23   12

7:27   94

7:34   114, 117

9:57-62   114

9:58   117

9:59-60   62

9:60   114-15

9:61-62   63

10:4   62, 115

10:7   62

10:9   67, 93

10:12   92

10:12-15   65

10:13   67

10:13-15   117

10:14   92

10:16   65

10:17   117

10:18   117

10:21   117

10:22   80

10:29-37   115

11:2   93

11:9-13   106, 118

11:17-22   117

11:19-20   67

11:20   11, 65, 93, 117

11:31-32   94

11:49-51   92

12:5   92

12:7   110

12:8-9   64, 90, 94

12:19-20   114

12:22-31   116, 118

12:35-38   94

12:39-46   94

12:42-46   92

12:49   92

12:51   115

12:51-53   94, 109

13:1-5   109-10

13:10-17   68

13:23-24   115

13:24   94

13:28-29   94

13:30   114-15

14:1-6   68, 114

14:11   93, 116

14:12-14   94

14:26   63, 115

14:27   63

14:33   63

15:11-32   106, 115

16:1-13   115

16:13   114

16:16   94

16:18   41, 62

16:19-31   56, 93

17:1-2   92

17:3-4   63

17:6   67

17:11-19   68

17:16   117

17:20   117

17:26-30   92

17:33   63, 93, 116

17:34-35   92

18:8   92

18:14   93, 116

19:1-10   116

19:11   95

19:26   93

21   100

21:34-36   94

21:38   44

22:28-30   65, 94

22:30   94

22:50-51   68

24   35

24:1-53   117

24:53   44

John

1:1   81

1:41   94

2:1-12   68

2:13-17   114

4:17-18   68

4:25   94

4:29   94

5:1-18   68

5:27   94

5:28-29	94	19:34	80	**Philippians**	
6:1-15	67	20–21	117	2:6-7	80
6:14-15	94	20:28	81	2:6-8	28
6:16-21	67	20:30	68		
6:40	93	21	100	**Colossians**	
7:36	44	21:20-23	95	1	52
7:53–8:11	43-44, 49	21:22-23	100	1:15-19	81
8:58	81	21:25	44		
9:1-12	68, 110			**1 Thessalonians**	
9:22	94	**Acts**		4:17	92
10:24	94	2:22	80		
11	68			**2 Timothy**	
11:27	94	**1 Corinthians**		4:8	84
11:35	80	7:10	62		
12:9	117	7:10-11	56	**Hebrews**	
13–17	100	9:14	62	5:8	80
14:2-3	93	13	27-28	13:2	51
14:6	86	13:4-5	28		
15:6	92			**2 Peter**	
17	86	**2 Corinthians**		3:1-10	100
18:15-18	117	4:18	113		
18:25-27	117	12:1-5	76	**Revelation**	
19:28	80			21:5-6	81

Printed in the USA
CPSIA information can be obtained
at www.ICGtesting.com
LVHW041215150324
774517LV00035B/1459